THE ART
AND SCIENCE OF
GRAND PRIX DRIVING

NIKI LAUDA

Motorbooks International
Publishers & Wholesalers Inc
Osceola, Wisconsin 54020, USA

This edition first published in 1977 by Motorbooks International Publishers & Wholesalers, Inc.

Formel I by Niki Lauda © 1975 by Verlag Orac, Vienna

Published in the United Kingdom under the title, *Formula 1, The Art and Technicalities of Grand Prix Driving*

English translation copyright © 1977 by William Kimber & Co. Limited, London

ISBN: 0-87938-049-7
Library of Congress Catalog Number: 77-13985

Library of Congress Cataloging in Publication Data

Lauda, Niki, 1949–
      The art and science of Grand Prix driving.

      Translation of Formel 1.
      1.   Lauda, Niki.   2.   Automobile racing drivers — Biography.   3.   Automobile racing.   4.   Automobiles, Racing.   I.   Title.
GV1032.L38A3313   796.7'2'0924 [B]   77-13985
ISBN 0-87938-049-7

Typeset by Watford Typesetters, Great Britain
Jacket and book printed and bound in the United States of America by The North Central Publishing Company, St. Paul

4   5   6   7   8   9   10

The collaboration of
Diplom-Ingeniuer Dr Fritz Indra
and Herbert Völker is gratefully acknowledged.

English translation : David Irving

Exclusive technical photographs : Heinz-Dieter Finck

Acknowledgments to Illustrations

Colour photographs: Carl Imber   Heinz-Dieter Finck   David Phipps
Alois Hans Rottensteiner   Martini
Black and white photographs: Heinz-Dieter Finck   Alois Hans Rottensteiner
D.P.P.I.   Ferdi Kräling   Roger Benoit   David Phipps   Carl Imber
UOP-Werksfoto   Ferrari-Werksfoto   Charles Loring   Jackie van Nimwegen
Erik della Faille   Werner Knorr   Jutta Fausel   Erwin Kneidinger
Augusto Baldoni   Popperfoto

Contents

FOREWORD

9

THE HUMAN ELEMENTS

11

TECHNICAL PRINCIPLES

Theory and practice – Basic facts on Formula I design and the theory behind them – The facts that determine how a car handles

TECHNICAL DATA

46

THE FORMULA I CAR'S COMPONENTS

48

and how to live with them – Monocoque and cockpit – Engine and gearbox – Tyres – Wheel suspension systems

DRIVING

103

Starting and warming-up – Driving off – Driving on the Straight – Cornering – Combination curves – The ten toughest bends on today's Grand Prix tracks

TESTING AND TRAINING

139

Ferrari's test track – Basic tests – Setting up the car – Tyre tests – Defects in recent years – Practice laps – Trying for Pole Position

THE RACE

165

The start – Racing Routine – Overtaking – Tactics – Changes in car, road surface and opponents – My finest race – My easiest victory – My most dangerous situation – My decision in Japan

FITNESS

222

Body-building – Recreation

IN THE MIDST OF LIFE

239

Foreword

When I was at the very beginning of my career there was one particular book that held a special fascination for me. Piero Taruffi wrote it some eighteen years ago. It was a serious survey of the theory and practice of his sport. For a young fan like me it provided the answers to hundreds of questions, and ever since then I have greatly valued this kind of book. Technology has, in the meantime, produced other cars and created different sets of conditions. And television has carried the interested individual right to the site of the action – where he can see a great deal but is not provided with much deeply informative explanation. Since the days of Taruffi the sport has become not only more intricate and manifold, but much more 'public' too. I could not resist the challenge of trying to describe these changed sets of factors in a book in which new questions would be raised and answered, with the emphasis on the side of my sport that is now really the most important – the technicalities that are generally hidden from the public by all the Grand Prix showmanship. I wanted to reveal and explain all the things that get the show on the road in the first place. Because if the subject is approached primarily from this angle, there is not much trace of show business left. What does remain is the fascination and the pleasure of those who have a job to do – whether at the drawing-board or behind the steering wheel.

NIKI LAUDA

The Human Elements

A Discussion with Herbert Völker

VÖLKER: To those of us who have been closely following your career one special moment seems particularly fascinating – the moment when you decided to take the plunge and incur a one-million Schilling debt in order to open up the way for the next stage of your career. At that moment you must have been dead certain within yourself that you were right out in front with the world's best drivers, otherwise it would have been madness to accept such a risky debt. But up to that moment you had had no opportunity of comparing yourself with, say, a Jackie Stewart racing the same cars. So where did you get your incredible self-confidence that told you : I've got it in me to be a super-star?

LAUDA: I had one vital opportunity to make comparisons, and that was racing with Ronnie Peterson during my Formula II season for March in 1971. At that time Ronnie was already the big new star and we practised on the same day in the same car. That was the last year that I had financial backers behind me. The year after that I had to take the big decision – to accept a one-million Schilling debt or to go back to Square One. Then there was that race at Rouen : I outbraked Ronnie at the chicane and overtook him, only to get the slow-down signal one lap later. I was so startled of course that I at once let Ronnie pass me again. But on that occasion Ronnie had put the wrong wings on his car, so I myself didn't rate my achievement half as high as the various test sessions where we were both driving the same car. He was faster than me and I kept asking myself : six-tenths of a second, where's he getting them from – there must be some explanation. After a time I hit on the logical answer and that's how I also cut off a few tenths of a second and then I was as fast as he was. The trouble was that in the race itself I was still three seconds slower because he had a good engine and I had a lame old animal that had already become notorious as the 065, which they say Jim Clark was driving right after the war.

VÖLKER : And after that comparison with Peterson you came to the conclusion : If I get a chance I'll get to the top?

LAUDA : Well yes, most of all I learned a hell of a lot from Ronnie. Driving flat out, taking risks, cutting off the tenths. And of course I realized one thing : on speed alone I've got him, I just need polish – and of course a real car too.

VÖLKER : Just as you were confident then you could match up to Ronnie would you today go so far as to say : I'm as fast as, or faster than, all the rest put together?

LAUDA : I know how to steer a car well, and when it's on course I know how to get the best out of it – how to drive so fast that I can state quite bluntly : you can't go faster.

VÖLKER : In other words faster than the rest?

LAUDA : No. All the top drivers go just as fast. There's only one line and you can only drift by a set amount from that line. If there's a guard rail you can drift to within an inch of it, but closer to that is just not on. And when you're outbraking them you cannot go beyond a certain point – otherwise you go off. So if my car's set up the same as the others I can't drive any faster than they can no matter who they are, because we are all driving flat out. If you've got six drivers who are all masters of this 'optimum' driving, then all six will be equally fast provided their cars are set up identically.

VÖLKER : So any difference there is between this handful of men will be in their cars and in their ability to get the best they can out of them.

LAUDA : That's it.

VÖLKER : And do you think you can set your car up for a given circuit better than anybody else?

LAUDA : No. But what I do know is that I work hard and concentrate every ounce of my ability on setting up my car.

VÖLKER : So : in 1971 you measured yourself against Peterson and recognized that you could be something special. What about right at the beginning of your career, did you have any inkling then that one day you'd become a world racing star?

LAUDA : No. In every class I set myself a limit – for instance, in mountain racing I have to be faster than Lemmy Hofer. If he'd beaten me just once then I would have had to give up. I had to flatten my own class, that was the first thing.

VÖLKER You've probably already heard the thesis and its countless variations that run like this : in all likelihood there are thirty people in India who can drive as well as Fittipaldi, but they just don't get the chance to show it. What do you say to that?

LAUDA : And then there are a hundred Karajans too – all mouldering down the mines! No, getting your own way is an indispensable part of being a success. You can only be a Fittipaldi if you've overcome all the obstacles that faced him, like making the journey from Brazil to Britain. When Fittipaldi became famous people began saying there was a man called Pace in Brazil who was even faster. So long as Mr Pace was racing Go-Karts and Fitti was driving the Lotus next to Jochen, Pace was of no interest. The talk about Pace only really started when he had got his way too and was over here. And then it turned out that he was only just as fast as Fittipaldi, but not any faster because you just can't be any faster. Besides driving fast is only one basic aspect of the good racing driver, it's only the first thing. A man can be king of the drivers but if he always chooses the wrong car or keeps making some silly mistake then he's not in the world class at all – no matter how fast he can drive.

VÖLKER : To follow this point through : then you ought not to have made the mistake of tying yourself for years on end to BRM and Louis Stanley?

LAUDA : I had no choice. That year the sponsor's money I was hoping for didn't materialize and Stanley put pressure on me : either I sign a long-term contract or I must come up with cash on the spot from a sponsor right that moment. So I went over to Ferrari. I knew my decision wasn't really fair to Stanley. But I knew for a cert that Stanley would never be able to put together a good team with BRM again. I didn't take that decision to leave because Ferrari was any better at that time. Ferrari had also hit rock bottom, but they did offer every prospect of a successful job. With BRM that wasn't the case. Taking that decision was an awful worry, because literally everything was at stake.

VÖLKER : But Lauda the Ace obviously took the right decision. To stick to the sport itself, to this 'optimum driving' : are there only four or five men who have the knack, or are there more?

LAUDA : There's no other way round. To get the best out of such a car you have to have been driving Formula I two years at least – and not just with any jerks either. But to get into Formula I at all and to get your hands on good cars you've got to be capable of more than just putting your foot down. If what you're talking about is 'talent', there are definitely more men with magnificent talent than there are men who today know how to drive a Formula I car flat out. Talent alone is not enough.

VÖLKER : In other words you don't think much of any organized talent-promotion?

LAUDA : Quite useless. Competitive driving is part of the story and no one can do without it. Racing-driver schools achieve something but only up to a point. After that you're on your own and have to fight your way to the front.

VÖLKER : Are you under stress?

LAUDA : Yes.

VÖLKER : But nobody is forcing you to work so hard. Aren't you perhaps too greedy?

LAUDA : I'm just earning money, that's all. I have to force myself to go to an autographing session. That's real hard labour and I admit I put a high price on it. And the good money has only recently started flowing.

VÖLKER : Is the money the most important thing for you in racing?

LAUDA : Not the most important, but still important.

VÖLKER : Assuming you only earned a hundred thousand Schillings a year from racing, so you could just scrape a living out of it : would you still be a racing driver or would you prefer to take a managerial job where you would earn two hundred thousand?

LAUDA : That's a hypothetical question that I can't answer. When I became a racing driver money meant nothing to me. It was the cars that fascinated me and even today working with cars is the job I dream of. It's a risky job, and I can earn money in it. That's what matters to me.

VÖLKER : Your price for an hour's autograph session is the same as a minor director earns in a month. Why do you ask for so much – you don't run much risk signing autographs!

LAUDA : That's one of the primitive laws of business life, that you take note of the market value. After all, the people wouldn't pay me so much if I wasn't worth it to them. And from my own point of view it makes more sense to earn x schillings for one hour than to work five hours for only a fifth of x.

VÖLKER : So we can say you work for what you can get. This is bound to put you into stress situations, obviously not because of the autograph sessions so much as because you can never really relax. And on top of that you have all the nervous strain of the races – doesn't it all get too much for you? Don't you ever see little white mice in your sleep?

LAUDA : There are evenings when I find it hard to get to sleep because I'm overstrung.

VÖLKER : What do you do about it?

LAUDA : First and foremost is to recognize such situations for what they are. Earlier I wasn't able to do that. Instead of relaxing after a race I would dash madly from one fixture to another until I was just dropping from sheer exhaustion. Today I have a grip on myself and act accordingly.

VÖLKER : No, those are quite normal situations that any man who works hard and thinks hard experiences. What I meant were situations in which the going got so tough that your mind started playing tricks on you. Has that ever happened?

LAUDA : Not very often.

VÖLKER : Nightmare days of crashes like the 1975 Barcelona Grand Prix or the 1976 Nürburgring, when you nearly lost your life, must surely leave a scar on your mind that's so deep that you can't stop thinking about it for a long time afterward?

LAUDA : It shakes me up, it does affect me, but it doesn't unbalance me. I can't allow it to overwhelm me, just as I must not be afraid or worry about it.

VÖLKER : But no man can control his emotions like fear, can he?

LAUDA : It's just a matter of will-power. You've got to develop a strong will and stubborn head, as well.

VÖLKER : This stubbornness – does one have it, or does it have to be developed first?

LAUDA : You've got it already and you can cultivate it. I can be insanely obstinate and an immense egoist as well.

VÖLKER : This obstinacy, or brutality perhaps, is it what really counts for the likes of you? Is everybody who has reached the top like that?

LAUDA : Yes, otherwise they couldn't keep on driving after seeing their first fatal crash. Because the point is otherwise bound to come when they say it's downright madness. You don't have to be a racing driver, there don't even have to be any race meetings.

VÖLKER : And this point doesn't come?

LAUDA : Perhaps it came from those who stopped racing. For those like me who're still driving it hasn't come. It can't have come otherwise we couldn't carry on with our chosen profession. Once in your lifetime you've got that decision : Do you want to practise this profession? Do you want it and all that that involves? If you ask yourself that question and if you answer in all honesty with yes, then that means you've beaten the problem – then you can't be afraid any more because if you are then you must have answered that question with a lie.

VÖLKER : Aren't there other racing drivers who are more sensitive than you?

LAUDA: No, at least not any good ones. They'd be frightened and they'd worry and they'd sleep badly and they'd be too slow.

VÖLKER When somebody begins racing he's usually too young and too immature to put such a vital question as that to himself. When you're eighteen you don't ask yourself questions, you just want to put your foot down on that pedal. Was there any one concrete moment of time when you put that question to yourself and gave yourself an answer?

LAUDA: Yes there was. It was 5 September 1970 – by coincidence it was the very day Jochen Rindt was killed.

VÖLKER: What do you mean, coincidence?

LAUDA: Jochen had nothing at all to do with it. It was pure chance, that I had my decisive experience on precisely the same day as Jochen died. I was at Zolder, Jochen was at Monza.

VÖLKER: How was that?

LAUDA: It was a Formula III race. That season I had already had four accidents. That formula was quite crazy anyway. There were 25 men, every one as fast as the other and none would give ground. You drove in formation over the brow of a hill at 120 mph and we were bumping into each other like the dodgem cars at the Prater in Vienna. You had to be mad to drive this formula. And was I mad! When I just think back to my very first Formula III race: I drove to the South of France by car with Pankl, a 36-hour drive to Nogaro with this transporter in tow. We were the only Austrians, lined up against thirty lunatic Frenchmen. First practice: I drop into Pankl's slipstream, let him suck me along and I'm about to pull out. At that moment his engine dies on him. My left front wheel collides with his right rear wheel, my car takes off, clears a track official, lands by the guard-rail, loses all four wheels and skids a hundred yards along the rail until there's virtually nothing left of the car worth speaking of. That was the end of my first five minutes driving Formula III, in my very first practice session.

VÖLKER: Didn't the spectre of that accident haunt you over the weeks that followed?

LAUDA: In that case I ought to have been haunted by three other accidents too. I was always taking off like that. We drove amok back to Vienna, I picked up a new chassis from McNamara, had a new car rapidly put together and drove off to the Nürburgring. There I was, in fifth place with nobody visible ahead of me and nobody behind either. In spite of that I ended up off the track and don't know to this day how it happened. Just like that! That was my second race and my second crash. Then we went to France again, again 36 hours by car.

There, I mix up the gear lever positions and change down instead of up: that was curtains for both the transmission and the engine. After that came Brands Hatch. Before the race the photographer Rottensteiner asks me which is the best curve. I tell him, in front of the pits, somebody's bound to fly off the track there – and I ask you! I'm trying to outbrake an opponent on the offside and I cut the corner and the other fellow hits my rear wheel so I fly right out – and right in front of Rottensteiner. The car was a write off. And then there was the race at the beginning of September at Zolder.

VÖLKER : What was special about that?

LAUDA : That was the maddest thing of all. Third lap: an accident – Hannelore Werner – somewhere on the track. We hit the brow of the hill in formation at 120 and that's when we find the crash-truck barely doing 30. The first three skidded past it to the right. Hunt made it, so did Birrell. Then another tried to pass on the right, he didn't quite make it and went into a spin. I'm now trying to pass on the left, meantime the other car's spinning to the left, we collide, I turn right round and the next car volleys straight into me. The whole scene takes place slap in the middle of the track, I'm standing there with my car in shreds when the next bunch of cars comes flying over the hill towards us. By now the yellow flag is up and there's all manner of signals, but that mob just kept their foot down. All I could do was sit tight and wonder which side I'd get shot down from first. One flew right over the nose of my car then I jumped out and got the hell out of there.

VÖLKER : And that race was your final experience like that?

LAUDA : Yes, that was an anti-race and it was the climax of something of an anti-season. After that I had a big think about the whole thing and came to the conclusion that while I did want to stay a racing driver, with all that meant, I didn't want to be a lunatic in a field of two dozen other lunatics. So I never got into another Formula III car but devoted all my energy to scraping together the money to buy my way into Formula II.

VÖLKER : And that one decision was what carried you over all the obstacles after that?

LAUDA : As far as choice of job was concerned, yes. After that I never doubted this was the right career for me and that in this job I would be able to employ my talents to the full. And what that implies, is that you're not allowed to feel fear. Take the Zeltweg circuit for instance, the Bosch Curve: you approach it at 175 mph, step on the brakes and skim past the guard-rail with only inches to spare. If at that instant you suddenly think of the possibility of a tyre defect or brake-damage then you shouldn't even start racing because you'll never get anywhere near your target. There'd always be shoals of problems, worries and anxieties that would keep occurring to you.

VÖLKER : And nothing like that ever occurs to you?

LAUDA : No, or I'd have chucked it all up long ago. Because it would have been pointless to brake ten yards too soon each time.

VÖLKER : Don't you need to do a kind of mental gymnastics to keep such 'evil thoughts' at bay?

LAUDA : No. You learn to switch off. I throw a switch in my brain, then I'm a racing driver and nothing else. A racing-driver without feelings, and hence without fear. Then you drive, and nothing 'occurs' to you. The big problem comes in finding how long it takes to switch back on again – in other words to change back from racing-driver to human being again.

VÖLKER : How long does it take you?

LAUDA : Relatively little time compared with other drivers. But things do happen that I wouldn't normally do. You meet people over-taut from the atmosphere of the race and you don't easily see eye to eye with them. For instance there was this track official in Canada who panicked when I flew off the track and just kept shouting 'Master-switch, master-switch!' He wanted me to switch off the master switch. I had everything under control and I told him quite calmly I just wanted to get my helmet off first. At that the man went off his rocker, grabbed at the car and of course switched on the fire-extinguisher instead and that went off. I was so bloody mad I thumped the man with my crash helmet – something I'd never normally do and I'm deeply sorry to have done, but my own mental switch was still pointing to 'Racing' and not to 'Niki'. Or after the Argentinian Grand Prix : I'm coming out of the drivers' quarters with Mariella and somebody pulls me round and shouts 'Photo' so I jumped on him as well.

VÖLKER : To get back to your season of crashes. You drove like a lunatic but by some miracle you survived : what has changed you into a sane man in the meantime?

LAUDA : I think these crashes are necessary for the career of any racing driver. What matters is whether you learn your lesson from them or not. There are people who were driving five years ago in Formula III and half killing themselves and they're still driving there and they're still going off the road.

VÖLKER : You're something of an example for many youngsters but definitely for adults too, who like to lose themselves in the fantasy world of the Grand Prix hero. Do you feel you're only responsible to yourself, or do you feel a wider, moral obligation to set a good clean example?

LAUDA : I've no time for people who set examples. Nobody set me one, and I don't think others should be set one either. I only know how to drive like a Lauda, I can't drive like a Rindt or a Stewart or anybody else. At most I could pick up a few little tips but it would be a waste of time for me to say : I'd like to be like this man or that. And that's why I can't see myself setting examples to others either.

VÖLKER : Even so you're in the nation's showcase and you must have some influence on your admirers. Do you act accordingly?

LAUDA : I try to behave decently. It's easy enough for me as I was well brought up and I'm used to good manners. I won't attract attention by rowdy behaviour or drunkenness because I would never behave rowdily and I hardly touch alcohol. And if the journalists go wild because I kiss Princess Grace's hand all I can say is : I thought nothing of it, it struck me as perfectly normal to kiss her hand as that's the way I have been taught.

VÖLKER : Wasn't your good upbringing a bit of a handicap for you? Didn't the luxury of your parental home turn you a bit soft?

LAUDA : As a child, quite definitely. Even when it wasn't all that cold I had to wear a scarf and coat and put on a Styrian hat. My brother was always identically dressed, we looked two complete nitwits. I can see it all so vividly still : there I am, eleven or twelve years old and paying frequent visits to the dentist who's straightening my teeth out. I'm standing with my mother on the corner by the Forum cinema waiting for the tram. I just keep looking at this manhole cover – each time a car goes over it it wobbles, click-clack. And if I visualize now how I must have looked standing there in my coat and scarf and hat on that corner – I must have looked a real *Seicherl*, a softy !

VÖLKER : What got you out of the softy rut?

LAUDA : I was dead crazy about cars. At fifteen I bought a 1949 Volkswagen for 1,500 Schillings. I was able to drive backwards and forwards in our back-yard. I did a new paint job with a spray gun and took its engine apart. Then I had it towed to my parents' estate where I could drive round the private roads in it. I built soil ramps for it and just about every contraption you can think of. Because of that car I needed a lot more cash than my pocket-money provided so I took on holiday jobs and at 16 I was working as a lorry driver's mate. Some-times he let me drive too. Ever since than I've been fascinated by lorries. I think I'd like to own a lorry one day. But to be a driver's mate I had to get up at one-thirty a.m. – and you can't be a softy after that.

VÖLKER : When you were taking your Volkswagen over the ramps at 15, did you have any ambition to be world champion? That must have been 1964, the year Surtees made world champion. Did you see yourself as John Surtees or as Niki Lauda, as you took those ramps?

LAUDA: As Lauda. I didn't want to be world champion, I always thought only of the next step. And the next step then was a driving licence, in three years' time.

VÖLKER: You just said you had no idols. But can I ask this: didn't you have a sneaking admiration for the heroes of that age, like Surtees?

LAUDA: My uncle took me once to Nürburgring and I saw Surtees there. He was already going grey-haired and that made quite a deep impression on me, though not for long.

VÖLKER: The one man dominating racing driving all those years was Jim Clark. How did he strike you?

LAUDA: At Easter 1968 I went to watch the meeting at Aspern, outside Vienna. Frank Gardner won in a Lotus-Cortina. Afterwards it was announced that Jim Clark had been killed in an accident at Hockenheim. For an instant I felt dreadfully sad. Not because I was sorry for him, somehow, no, I just thought that now we would miss him. That he had just gone like that, that hurt.

VÖLKER: Did you feel the same way about Rindt?

LAUDA: No, I was just very depressed.

VÖLKER: As you said earlier that was on the same day as your crash at Zolder. When there's a coincidence like that, surely that ought to motivate you to give it all up and not precisely the contrary?

LAUDA: It gave me food for thought and a fixed viewpoint that I didn't feel compelled to re-analyze after that.

VÖLKER: Did Jochen Rindt get under your skin?

LAUDA: Yes. Not that I knew him at all well. I only met him a couple of times quite briefly. But if I see his photos now it makes me tingle. He had a good head. He looked like somebody who was somebody. He had real class, at least I felt he had.

VÖLKER: Would you say Rindt had a broader public following than you do today?

LAUDA: That I can't say. There's no way of making comparisons here. Not with Rindt while he was alive, anyway. Don't get me wrong on that, but to be killed and then become world champion – there's never been a situation like it and that's why there's no way of holding up a yardstick to Rindt.

VÖLKER: That being a star isn't all roses becomes very clear the more you think about it. You're public property and your privacy is repeatedly violated while on the other hand you have enormous privileges and the feeling that millions admire and envy you. How would you rate the pros and cons of popularity?

LAUDA: Whether it's a matter of queueing for something or getting a fine, I do get red-carpet treatment. I don't like waiting, so these privileges are very welcome to me. Obviously it does happen though not often, that somebody says: I say Lauda ought to be able to wait his turn like the rest of us, and I say of course I can wait, I didn't ask for special treatment, they offered it to me. But even here in everyday life it's success that counts: if I'm a Niki Lauda who's been having a run of defeats then this is the first place I get to know it. But if I've just won three Grand Prix the people fall over themselves to please me. To take the disadvantages first, you can take things out of context and say Lauda is arrogant. But you've got to look at the whole picture and the truth is, unfortunately, that people do get on my nerves. The worst of all is on race weekends where you're up to your eyes with your own problems anyway and over and above that you're supposed to sign autographs, answer stupid questions and you don't get a moment to yourself. You've got a day of practice behind you, that has left you a nervous wreck and what you need now is rest and relaxation, you get back that evening to your hotel and there you find thirty men waiting for you, grabbing you, barring your way, asking for signatures, again and again and again. Monte Carlo is the worst. After the race you get claustrophobia. We had a steel rail left and right of our pits, holding back thousands of Italians whose only desire was to shake my hand, hug me, or pull me apart from sheer excitement. If you don't watch out you'll get torn apart. I have to put up with things there that anybody else would define as a bodily assault. For instance somebody snatches my cap. Don't get me wrong – I couldn't care less about the cap, I've given away hundreds of them to people who asked me for them. But in that instant when somebody brutally tugs off your cap you just see red – what gives that bastard the right to treat me like that? Maybe it is the highest token of admiration, I don't care: to me it's assault and theft. In a situation like that at Monaco your only bet is to scream for help and that's just what I did. The mechanics just drove through the mob with a van and literally liberated me.

VÖLKER: We both once drove back from Modena and wanted to get a cup of coffee in Innsbruck. At 11 p.m. we went into a pub and the people broke out into spontaneous applause. Are you pleased by that or does it get on your nerves?

LAUDA: It annoys me. I just want to go in and get a coffee or unwind a bit. And I don't want to have to tell everybody: Thank-you. Why should I? I keep finding myself in situations that I haven't asked for. What I want is coffee; what I get is a storm of applause, everybody stares at me and expects me to give them a friendly grin. Who wants to spend his life giving friendly grins? I don't.

VÖLKER : So it doesn't boost your inner ego when people applaud?

LAUDA : No, it just embarrasses me.

VÖLKER : But no doubt there was a time in your career when it was very welcome to you?

LAUDA : Oh yes, right at the start. Somebody recognizes you : 'You're Lauda, aren't you?' At first I used to like it. But then you get to a point where there's nothing you want more than just a bit of peace and quiet, not because you are arrogant in any way, but because you just can't stand the hullabaloo any more. The constant tension – 'Look, they're looking at you!' – and interruptions of your private life stop you being a normal human being. And it's the same with the journalists. Obviously when you're only a small Formula III driver you're pleased to get into the newspapers. But today I couldn't care less how often I'm mentioned in the press, I've seen it all before. I only read the newspapers to check that they haven't written rubbish about me, lies that I ought to defend myself against. I get angry when someone attacks me and there's nothing I can do about it.

VÖLKER : For instance?

LAUDA : Take all that hullabaloo about the Nürburgring. On the evening before the race I'm sitting watching TV and hear the man scoffing that I am yellow – raising the question whether the Nürburgring is too difficult for me and points like that. He doesn't go into the technical angles at all, just holds me up as some kind of funk. And I'm sitting there knowing ten million people are watching with me and I'm sitting here quite defenceless and can't defend myself. And then there was that time after my crash at Nürburgring in 1976. Blood-sucking photographers clung around like leeches for a week to get pictures of my horribly mutilated face. The hospital and especially my room were tightly cordoned off but one of them still got in. I was completely immobilized and couldn't even scream and there's this fellow standing at my bedside zooming in on me with his movie camera. You just can't describe what a shock a foul trick like that is to you.

And another example : I decided, a few weeks after the accident, to resume my public appearances. To me it seems quite normal for a man to pursue his career if he's still all in one piece, even if his face isn't a picture any more. It's not as though I'm going in for a beauty contest. It's what every cripple hopes for – to be treated like a normal human being by his fellow men again. If society denies him that it is downright brutal. If a one-armed man comes up to me the first thing I say to him isn't : 'What a sight you are ! What have you done with your arm, then ?' I would treat him like any other human being. Why do people treat me any differently? Why do people lose all their tact when they deal with Niki Lauda? Ought I to stay at home like a hermit for half a year? It would not be natural, and that is why it strikes me as quite normal to go back to my job. If I give journalists answers like : 'I just need my accelerator foot, who needs a face !' then you must realize that these are just natural reactions to the stupid and tactless questions that reporters ask. Aren't I ashamed to show my face in public, and dozens of other such questions. . . . In fact there are only two ways of taking all this : either you go and hang yourself, because you feel ugly and unwanted or you give the kind of answer that the questioner deserves. And then they go and say, 'What a brute that Lauda is, giving answers like that.' But nobody talks about the callousness of the reporters and many other people. Evidently they assume that Lauda is a public animal and has to put up with anything that people say to him. I have got to learn to live with it, and I think that I know how.

VÖLKER : You once said you felt it was your duty to please your fans, to give them what they want. Do you still say that ?

LAUDA : Basically yes, so long as I am able to. But it's not getting any easier now. If they won't give you one minute during a race weekend without signing autographs, it does get on top of you. Just imagine, all you want is bed and sleep and in the hotel foyer there's a mob of people you've got to fight and autograph your way through. The point's bound to come when I say : that's the lot. You can't even work in peace, I can't even talk with a mechanic without somebody thrusting a scrap of paper under my nose to sign. Certainly it's a part of my job to sign autographs, perhaps even thousands of them a month. As you know I always answer written requests for autographs and when a firm pays through the nose for an hour's autograph session then I have to give them their money's worth.

VÖLKER : Helmut Zwickl once coined the phrase that there's a 'new race' of racing drivers. What he meant by that was the generation of racing-driver automats who only knew how to get the best out of their cars but degenerated to little more than specialists in the process. You must have had a wide and varied upbringing, but it must be several years since you went to the theatre or read a book. Is that right ?

LAUDA : Yes and more's the pity. I can't help noticing that a part of me is going to waste. I keep myself informed on current world affairs but that's about the sum total of it. In the evening I'm not up to reading any more.

VÖLKER : Don't you think that's a worry? Aren't you missing out on things?

LAUDA : It's pointless to brood on it. If I tried to widen my horizons I'd have to neglect my career, and that might be fatal.

VÖLKER : What part does your wife play in your career?

LAUDA : I try to keep my career and private life separate as far as possible. In my job that's not always 100 per cent possible, so Marlene does get drawn into the hurly-burly. And she's magnificent at it: she's a help and a support to me without coercing me in any way, and that's something that means a lot to me. I found Marlene's attitude after my bad Nürburgring crash in August 1976 particularly splendid: any other wife would have taken the opportunity to talk me out of going on racing. Not Marlene! It's largely thanks to her that I got back on my feet again, and there was never a word from her about my giving it all up.

VÖLKER : How do you imagine that you might still one day give it all up? What'd be the cause of such a retirement?

LAUDA : If this sport lost its interest for me.

VÖLKER : Do you think such a moment would ever come?

LAUDA : No.

VÖLKER : Have you any idea what you'd do after retiring?

LAUDA : I'd only do things I liked doing. Flying, for instance. Perhaps I'd make flying my career. To me there's nothing better than flying. To be in full control of a Jumbo jet – that would be the ne plus ultra for me.

Technical Principles

This section, for which I am indebted to Dr Fritz Indra, is an introduction to the technical factors of Formula I. It highlights the points that are of importance in the cars' construction, and give the unmechanically-minded reader a better understanding of the chapters that follow. For the purpose of better readability theoretical factors have been set out in this introduction in a much simplified form. Thus in many descriptions precise technical terms have been avoided so as to aid a general understanding. The purists might like to bear this in mind.

RULES OF THE GAME

Every sport has its rules of the game. In motor racing, these rules are laid down by the FIA (Fédération Internationale de l'Automobile). Formula I is in a manner of speaking the top of the league and enjoys most latitude in its design, as it has the fewest technical restrictions. At the moment the regulations are those in force from early 1966 to the end of 1979. Such alterations as there have so far been in this period concerned only safety regulations, in which connection the limitation on aerodynamic aids ('wings') was the biggest change to the external picture of the sport.

    These are the main regulations that the designer has to observe :
- a single-seater racing car with at least four wheels
- minimum weight 575 kilograms
- engine of no more than twelve cylinders and 3 litres, running on commercial Super petrol. If the full 3 litre capacity is used than supercharging is prohibited; this is only permitted in engines up to 1.5 litres, but in practice no racing stable uses it although Renault has now built such an engine
- at no point is the body width to exceed 140 centimetres; there is no limit on length but the overall width must not exceed 215 centimetres. The front

wing must not exceed 150 centimetres in width while the rear wing is restricted to 110 centimetres, and every designer uses these widths down to the last millimetre

O maximum petrol tank capacity of 250 litres (55 gallons) to be distributed between several tanks, each holding no more than eighty litres (17.6 gallons).

The rules of the game are most stringent where they apply to oil and petrol tanks.*

THE POINTS THAT COUNT IN RACING CARS

All the engines used in Formula I are pretty much the same as far as their characteristics are concerned. At the moment five engines meet the Formula I specifications : the eight-cylinder engine by Ford-Cosworth that has dominated the scene for years, and the twelve-cylinder engines by Ferrari, Alfa-Romeo, BRM and Matra. Since all these engines have virtually identical power outputs when they have been properly assembled and tuned, namely from 475 to 500 horsepower, the technological rivalry flourishes more around the car's handling than its engine power. So we shall discuss the criteria relating to the car's handling first in this technical introduction.

We must begin with the actual contact patch, that is the small area of contact between the tyre and the road surface. The car can only be made to move by means of such force as can be transmitted through the contact patches. As cogs and gears do not come into it, the transfer of energy into motion can only be achieved by friction – the better the grip afforded by the two contact surfaces and the greater the force holding them together, the more the energy that can be thus transferred.

The tyres have to transfer not only the drive forces but also braking and centrifugal forces – naturally under the same laws of friction. If the friction is entirely used up in one direction, as for example if a wheel locks when the brakes are applied, this locks it in the other directions too : in other words the tyres cannot accept any other forces and the car cannot be controlled any more. Normally the tyres have to put up with a combination of stresses : lateral and longitudinal forces will each be involved. Then according to circumstances – driving on the straight or round a curve – the one or the other component will come to the fore : on the straights the tyres are transferring almost exclusively

* For the precise wording of these regulations see the FIA Handbook, published by Patrick Stephens, Cambridge.

longitudinal forces with minor lateral forces caused by sidewinds or track irregularities. When cornering, you cannot exploit the full lateral friction as you need longitudinal forces too in order to keep up your speed and to be able to accelerate.

HOW FAST SHOULD CURVES BE TAKEN?

Cornering ability is without doubt one of the most vital characteristics deciding the qualities of a racing car. So let us just go over the steps a designer must take to get things right in this connection.

The starting point is again the tyre/road contact. As we said, the better the grip afforded by the two contact surfaces and the greater the force holding them together, the more the energy that can be transferred.

A word first about the two contact surfaces: The road surface, with its good or bad grip qualities, is going to be a constant and the same for everybody. The forces that a tyre can accept on any given road surface are expressed in terms of a friction coefficient.

Friction Coefficient

The friction coefficient is a function of the tyre's characteristics (design, profile, rubber mixture, air pressure, aspect-ratio, rim width, diameter), its temperature and its rolling speed. The maximum value calculated for this coefficient in Formula I tyres today is 1.4. What this means in practice is that such tyres are capable of transferring forces of acceleration amounting to 1.4 times G, the acceleration due to gravity. By way of illustration: much higher friction coefficients are possible with exceptional special tyres like those used for example in American drag-racing. A dragster tyre need not have a long life at all and only has to transfer longitudinal forces, virtually, and it can catapult a suitable vehicle forwards at an acceleration of three times G. And that is ten times the acceleration ability of a normal production-line sports car.

Slip Angle

The optimum friction coefficient can only be attained if the tyre's angle deviates slightly from the axis of travel. This angle of deviation is known as the angle of slip. Driving on the straight the angle of slip is in theory zero (though minimal values do in fact occur, due to toe-in and any side-winds). Even on normal curves the car does not follow exactly the angle set by the wheels, but drifts imperceptibly outwards. Therefore the front wheels have to be – equally imperceptibly – turned in an additional amount in order to be able to follow the curve. The angle of slip is thus the angle between the direction of the wheels (including the rear wheels) and the direction of travel. The familiar under- and oversteering characteristic can be expressed in terms of these two angles of slip (i.e., front and rear) : if the angle is greater at the front axle than at the back axle, then the car is under-steering.

In normal motoring large angles of slip are never or at best only seldom used, but the whole art of racing driving depends on taking corners with the angles of slip that yield the highest friction coefficients. If these optimum angles are exceeded, then the frictional forces fall off again. This explains why a car that is driven sideways may well look very spectacular but it is not moving at its best.

With the radial tyres on saloon cars these optimum angles of slip are quite large, 10 or 15°; with the broad Formula I racing tyres they are only about half as big. That is why properly driven saloon cars will drift more strongly than properly driven Formula I cars. We recall the statement made earlier that the forces that can be transferred depend on the character of the contact surfaces (the friction coefficient) and the force that holds them together. This latter force, operating vertically downwards, is known as the wheel loading.

Wheel loading

When static, a vehicle's wheel loading is a function of the centre of gravity's position and the all-up weight of the vehicle. In modern Formula I cars the weight distribution between front and rear is 40 : 60, i.e. 20 per cent of the all-up weight rests on each front wheel and thirty per cent on each rear wheel. But this holds true only for the vehicle at rest : the moment it moves off, the static wheel loadings are subjected to dynamic influences for instance by acceleration (higher wheel loadings in the rear) or by braking (higher wheel loadings in the front) or by taking curves (higher wheel loadings on the outside wheels). Whatever these displacements, however, the sum total of the four wheel-loadings will remain constant – it is only affected by the car's aerodynamics. This brings us to the importance of the aerodynamic aids (wings) that increase the downward pressure of the tyres on the road surface. The powerful effect when a car is strongly forced downwards (or even attracted downwards) is visible in the example of the little Slot Racing toy cars. An ingenious brain hit on the idea of installing a hidden magnet in the car, which helped it cling to the rails and attain astonishing speeds on the curves. The wings increase wheel-loadings to such an extent that nowadays a car without these aids would not have a chance in a Grand Prix race. On the other hand these wings do have an inherent danger: if a wing or its mounting snaps the car may be unable to handle its speed at that moment and it will go out of control.

In practice the theories relating to the best shape of the various aerodynamic aids (noses, rear wings) are interpreted in a variety of ways (see the photographs following page 38). The relationship between wheel loading and frictional forces is not a linear one, and it is an important characteristic for all vehicle design problems. The graph of this quantity is known as the Tyre Characteristics Curve, and a rough indication of this is shown in the diagram.

Anti-roll bar

By means of the anti-roll bar it is possible – within certain limits – to carry out rapid displacements of wheel loadings. Every Formula I car has an anti-roll bar on both the rear and the front axle. The anti-roll bar is a torsion bar lying in the car's body right next to the axle concerned and parallel to it. It is mounted so that it can rotate in its two fastenings which are as close to the outside of the

Tyre Characteristics

The force on a racing car's front axle may be 200 kg, in other words 100 on each wheel. The diagram shows that then each tyre can individually accept 150 kg lateral force or the front axle can accept 300 kg lateral force. But if the entire axle load falls on one wheel, for instance should the inside wheel leave the ground when taking a curve thus shifting all 200 kg to the outside wheel, it is apparent from the graph that the acceptable lateral force is then only 250 kg which means that the car is not capable of taking that curve so fast.

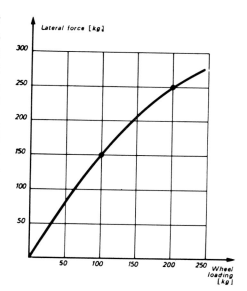

chassis as possible. It is operated by two lever arms connected by means of links to moving parts of the wheel suspension. Wheel movements up and down are transmitted by this means to the torsion bar. If these movements are equal on both right and left, for example when traversing a linear bump at right angles, the anti-roll bar does not operate – because of course no wheel-loadings are shifted. It begins to operate when the chassis rolls or when only one wheel moves up or down. Its mode of operation is simple : the anti-roll bar is under torsion during such movements. Depending on the thickness of the anti-roll bar (interchangeable) and the length of the lever arms (adjustable) it will offer more or less resistance to this torsion. By means of these variations deliberate wheel-loading displacements can be effected, which will influence a car's handling characteristics.

Let us see how the anti-roll bar can be used to influence the handling, using an under-steering example.

An under-steering car, of course, is one that tends to drift with its front wheels outside the curve : it is reluctant to enter the curve. In other words in comparison with the rear axle the front axle is accepting too little of the lateral forces. There are two possibilities of offsetting this effect : either we increase the lateral force on the front axle, or we diminish that on the back axle. So what we do is this : by softening the front anti-roll bar we transmit more load to the inside wheel (i.e., because of the softer anti-roll bar this wheel will not be relieved of as much load as before, thus it is in a position to accept more lateral force). This logically reduces the loading on the outer wheel. The total effect will be, as is plain from the tyre characteristics curve, that the whole axle will be able to accept more lateral force and thus the car's tendency to under-steer will be reversed. But that is not the only reason for change in the car's handling, because when the front anti-roll bar is softened the result is a torsion effect that is transmitted through the car's body and thereby affects the rear anti-roll bar too. This distorts the rear anti-roll bar more, diminishing the wheel loading on the inside and increasing it on the outside – with the overall result that the lateral force on the rear axis is diminished : and lower lateral force in the rear defeats under-steering just as surely as greater lateral force in the front.

Of course this double effect would only fully work out if there was such a thing as a perfectly rigid car body. And this is not possible because of course all materials are more or less elastic and there is no reason why a racing car should be any different. But the designer must nevertheless try, while holding down the car's overall weight, to build the body as rigidly as possible. And this is why the monocoque (shell) construction is preferable to the frame. It is possible to draw conclusions about the rigidity of a given car from the way it reacts to an anti-roll bar. Of course a car could be helped to handle normally even with anti-roll bars, just by changing the relationship of the rear and front wheel springs to each other. By hardening the springs all round the tendency to roll can also be reduced. But despite the minor weight benefits resulting from discarding the anti-roll bars there are disadvantages too. In a car without anti-roll bars all the springs must be that much harder, if it is to roll on curves by the same amount as a car with anti-roll bars. This will make the car altogether harder – it will not take ground ripples in its stride but will tend to skim over them and if the car loses ground contact for even only a short time as a result it will not be able to brake, accelerate or take corners so well. So the anti-roll bar permits a car with an otherwise soft basic springing to keep the tendency of the body to roll under control.

The anti-roll bar also takes part in an interplay that is a product of the suspension systems special to Formula I.

Why Wishbones?

In all Formula I cars only one suspension system is employed : independent suspension on double wishbones both front and rear. Without doubt this design is a good compromise between weight (unsprung weight), costliness and usefulness.

This suspension system derives from a time when much narrower tyres were used, quite simply because the enormous cost of designing new tyres did not appear to justify the effort. The broad tyres used today, which can accept greater acceleration, braking and lateral forces, highlight the system's inadequacies much more clearly.

Against the wishbone suspension speaks the fact that the wheel's presentation to the road surface (its camber) alters when it bumps or droops on one side or both sides. (If the camber is zero, this means the wheel's axis is parallel to the road surface; a positive camber means 'bandy legs', a negative camber means 'knock-knees'.

A wheel's camber has a considerable effect on a car's road handling, particularly if it changes during the drive. These changes are even more significant, the broader the tyre. In principle we can say, the more the camber the greater the lateral force but the higher the tyre temperature on the inside edge and thus the greater the wear. For this reason the very broad rear tyres in particular only permit cambers of at most 20 minutes of a degree (negative). The best thing would be if this camber could be retained under all circumstances (bump or droop on one or both sides), we could then speak of a constant camber. But this is only possible with solid rear axles and for design reasons these are right out of the question.[1] The very special De-Dion[2] rigid rear axle variation is the only alternative to the variable camber designs used so far. Such wheels always retain constant camber and would in principle be thinkable in Formula I; and Ferrari did begin in mid-1975 development work along these lines.[3]

But for the time being we make do with wishbones and so we have to live with the variable camber.

Camber changes

If the wheels on both sides of one axle lift by the same amount, the camber of both wheels alters by a negative amount. If the wheels lift or droop unequally (cornering, in other words the car rolls) then the camber of the more important outer wheel (important, because it takes the heavier load) alters by a positive amount while the camber of the less important inner wheel alters to negative. The extent of these alterations can be influenced by the positioning and lengths of the wishbones. An optimum adjustment for both cases (i.e., simultaneous and alternate spring movements) is not possible, only a compromise can be attained. For example if we want the wheel camber to remain constant when the springs move on the same side, the wishbones must be equal in length and parallel (parallelogram suspension). But this case is very unfavourable for taking curves as the entire roll of the body, about three degrees, is then transmitted to both wheels. In practice we prefer the position of the more important outer wheel to remain virtually unchanged when taking curves and accept the fact that when there is simultaneous spring movement there will be greater camber variations. For a given suspension geometry the effect of the wheels' springing can be better understood by setting up the following examples (we must bear in mind that

[1] Too much all-up weight because of the rigid and bulky axle, too much unsprung weight (axle plus differential), excessive chassis length (because a propellor shaft would be necessary).
[2] The De-Dion axle is in fact heavier than the wishbone axle, but nowhere near as heavy as a normal solid axle. The differential is rigidly attached to the engine and gearbox, the transmission of power to the wheels at each side is achieved by drive shafts, as with the wishbone axle.
[3] The first requirement was the T-gearbox. Only the economic use of space afforded by the diagonal installation provided a logical accommodation for the element linking the two wheel suspensions. This linkage can be effected either by the well-known De-Dion tube or a system of rigid struts.

My Ferrari B3 at Watkins Glen in 1974. The picture clearly demonstrates the dynamics of a Grand Prix car pushed to the limit. The car is taking a right-hand bend, as the three-degree roll of the body shows. The car's left hand wheels are compressing the springs eight centimetres more than those on the right. Although the car has been set up with high front roll stiffness, as is evident from the lifting of the inner front wheel, it is over-steering: the front wheels are turned away from the curve. The extreme lateral forces are forcing the tyres on the outer wheels sideways on their rims (especially clear here on the left rear wheel: it will be seen that the tread is no longer in the centre of the tyre). This frontal view also shows the difference in size of front and rear tyres, and how much of the car's cross-section is taken up by the aerodynamic nose and rear wing.

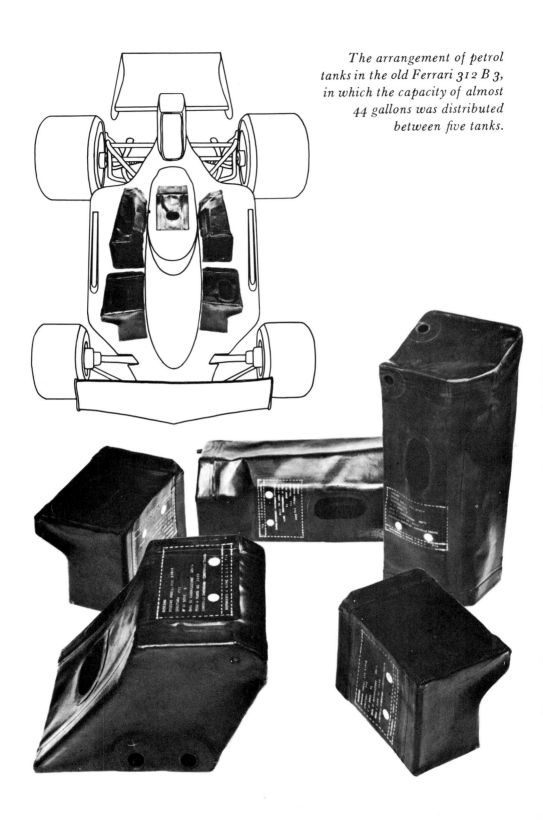

The arrangement of petrol tanks in the old Ferrari 312 B 3, in which the capacity of almost 44 gallons was distributed between five tanks.

an alteration of the camber of the front and particularly the rear wheels by only a fraction of a degree will suffice to affect the whole character of the car) :

1. The car is sprung as hard as possible : the resulting bump and droop movement of the wheel barely alters the camber, but the car is dumpy and skitters over road irregularities.

2. the car is fitted with anti-roll bars as hard as possible : it barely rolls on curves, so there is again little camber change, but the car is not in good contact with the road and steers badly.

Hardening the car like this is one rapid way of overcoming camber changes. To obviate the disadvantages described, extensive changes must be made to the suspension geometry (adjustments to wishbone lengths and repositioning the mounting points respectively).

Roll Axis

The position and length of the wishbones determine one of the most important concepts in vehicle construction, the roll centre. This is the point about which the car body moves under the influence of lateral forces. This point is constantly shifting by small amounts, since it depends on the movements of the wishbones. The roll centre is constant in two dimensions : it is fixed longitudinally in the car's centre, and at right angles to that in the centre of the roll axis. From the intersection of these two planes we obtain a perpendicular line passing through the differential on the back axle. The third dimension is its height : how high or low and roll centre lies (and it can even be 'below' the road's surface) and how much it lifts when the spring compression alters, are the factors that characterize the different suspension designs.

The notional line joining the roll centres on the back and front axles is the Roll Axis. This axis does not run parallel to the road surface; in modern design practice it tilts forwards, in other words the front roll centre is low (usually beneath the road surface) while the rear one is somewhat higher[1] (at about surface level or slightly above it). An expert can tell from a glance at the wishbones whether a car's roll centres are high or low. This is best demonstrated by the two sketches on page 36.

The various wishbone arrangements (and hence the various heights of roll

[1] The reason for this is that the broad rear wheels react more vigorously to camber changes than the front wheels. With the higher roll centre in the rear we can lessen the camber change on the rear axle when cornering.

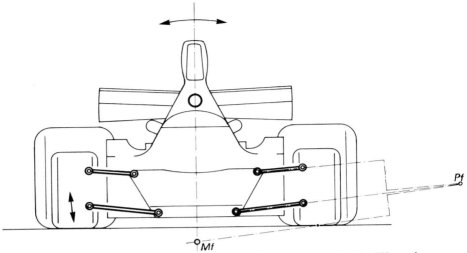

Lines projected through the two front wishbones intersect at point P_f. Thus the left front wheel will move around this point on its springs. Another line from point P_f through the wheel's point of road contact will cut the car's centre at M_f, thus giving the front roll centre. It is around this point that the car body will roll when taking corners.

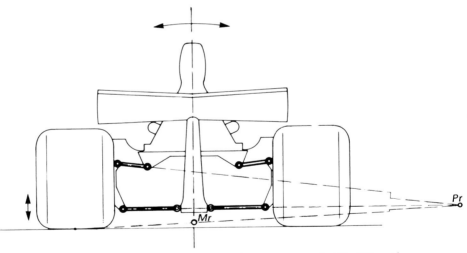

Lines projected by the two rear left wishbones intersect at point P_r. Thus the left rear wheel will move around this point on its springs. Another line from point P_r, passing through the wheel's point of road contact, will cut the car's centre at M_r, thus giving the rear centre of moment. It is around this point that the car body will roll when taking corners.

centres) have in modern racing practice little room for play; we find that all the cars adopt similar solutions, it is just a matter of subtle modifications.

Interactions

To recapitulate : camber changes are inevitable, but we must keep them as small as possible, whatever we do. Either we must mess around with the springing, or with the roll centres or with the body roll. There is not much joy to be had from the springing, so we must turn to the anti-roll bar that offsets the roll tendency. This is what becomes our main weapon for influencing the car's handling. The harder we set the anti-roll bar, the less the roll and the less the undesirable camber change too. But the driver now loses some of the feel of the car, so the anti-roll bar in fact has to be adjusted to leave him some of the feel without the camber changes becoming so big as to be downright unpleasant.

This interaction of anti-roll bar and camber can be demonstrated in three examples :

The vehicle is particularly 'sensitive' when a movement of the anti-roll bar is supported in its effect by the camber change caused by the vehicle's roll, in other words when the two tendencies are mutually supporting. This is the optimum case, this is a simple and easily adjusted vehicle from which we need fear no nasty surprises.

The second possibility is that anti-roll bar and camber cancel each other out in their effect. There is no easy way of making reasonable adjustments to the car, so we would have to make basic alterations to the wheel geometry.

Even worse is variation number three : when the effect of the camber change is greater than that of the anti-roll bar, because then the car will react 'against' the anti-roll bar. Take an example, the car is over-steering : normally we counteract this by softening the rear anti-roll bar, but in this case we accomplish precisely the opposite; because of the camber change's effect, the over-steering is only aggravated. In other words, we would have a very nasty car on our hands indeed.

But now we must recall that the origins of this interplay between anti-roll bar and camber lie in the car's roll and in the shortcomings of its suspension design. We have already discussed the suspension design, so now we will investigate how far the roll factor has to be taken into consideration even at the design stages of a racing car.

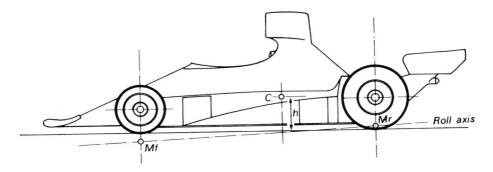

The line joining the front and rear roll centres is the roll axis. When centrifugal forces occur, the car body will begin to roll about this notional line. Centrifugal force is to be regarded as acting on the centre of gravity, C. The degree of roll will be proportional to the centrifugal force times the distance between the centre of gravity and the Axis roll axis, and inversely proportional to the hardness of the stabilizers and the springing.

Roll

How far a car rolls when taking corners depends on several factors:
○ the centrifugal force (which must always be regarded as acting on the centre of gravity);
○ distance between the car's centre of gravity and its roll axis (this distance is the 'lever arm' by which the centrifugal force acts);
○ anti-roll bars and springing as mutually counteracting components;
○ reaction of the wheels on the car body via the suspension.

If the 'lever arm' is reduced (by shortening the distance between the centre of gravity and the roll axis) the car will roll less. In the limiting case where the axis of roll coincides exactly with the centre of gravity – which we could easily accomplish by raising the roll centres[1] – the car will not roll at all. If we raise the roll axis *above* the centre of gravity something rather curious happens: the car does not roll outwards but inwards, when taking curves, with the driver sitting as though in a bucket seat on a merry-go-round. Not that the driver would have anything to laugh about: with such high roll centres the simultaneous raising or dropping of one pair of wheels would result in such camber

[1] I.e., by altering the wishbone positions the wishbones would have to incline upwards and inwards.

changes[1] that the tyres would be running on the outer shoulder one moment and on the inner shoulder the next – the car would turn crazy.

Of course raising the roll axis to such an extent is pure theoretical humbug. It is much more to the point to lower the centre of gravity to the (already low) roll axis, in other words to hold the centre of gravity as low as possible. This is a practical way of reducing the 'lever arm' on which the centrifugal force acts, and thus reducing the roll too. But we have already stated that a degree of roll is necessary in order not to lose the feel of a car, in order to be able to drive by feel. This small degree of deliberate roll can be obtained either by a softer basic springing or by means of softer anti-roll bars.

But lowering the centre of gravity is not only important for the roll of a car. And this brings us to an aspect that is the alpha and omega of racing car design.

The Height of the Centre of Gravity

The enormous importance of the height of the centre of gravity for racing car design derives from the transfer of loads from one wheel to another. Again we must consider the centrifugal force as acting on the centre of gravity. The size of the centrifugal force, coupled with the distance between the centre of gravity and the road surface, is what determines these changes in wheel loadings. This holds true both in the lateral and the longitudinal directions.

Quite apart from the reduction in roll already dealt with, the advantages of a low centre of gravity are these :

O the lower the centre of gravity, the less the load is shifted from the inner to the outer wheels when the car is cornering : we must recall the tyre diagram (page 29), from which it emerges that the optimum condition is a wheel loading distribution that is as equal as possible.

O the lower the centre of gravity, the less the load is shifted from rear to front when the brakes are applied. Again in the cause of a more equal load distribution we thus attain better braking effects : the rear wheels can be given a larger part in the braking process. If the centre of gravity is high up the load would, to put it in simple terms, tilt forwards and virtually all the brake effort would have to be done by the front wheels, because the 'lightened' rear wheels could transmit only a little braking force to the road surface.

---

[1] Of course it would also result in changes in the track width, and that would not do any good at all.

o the low centre of gravity does however have one disadvantage, though not a very serious one : when accelerating from a standing start or from low speeds, the load displacement to the rear wheels is less. As distinct from the braking process, when we want all four wheels to 'work' equally, for the optimum acceleration it would be most favourable if as much load as possible is brought to bear on the driving wheels, in other words on the rear axle. On the other hand if we had a *four*-wheel drive, the low centre of gravity would even be an advantage during the acceleration process.

Let's set up another purely theoretical example : suppose the centre of gravity coincided with the actual road surface, then taking corners, braking and accelerating would not result in any changes in wheel loading at all[1], in other words the static load distribution would always remain unchanged. In this case we would have optimum cornering, optimum braking, moderate acceleration. Of course as our car has got to lie on the road surface and not in it, all this is impossible. . . . But the example does help us to make our point : the lower the centre of gravity the faster we can take corners and the better we can brake. There is in fact a linear connection between them. For example, if the centre of gravity is lowered by half, the load shift resulting from centrifugal forces, from the inner to the outer wheels, is only half as great. The inner wheels can act more positively, the lateral control of the car becomes altogether greater. Naturally it is impossible for us to lower the centre of gravity to only half the height of that in a rival product, but even a few centimetres are enough to improve our prospects.

The Engine's Centre of Gravity

The Ferrari 312 T affords a good example of consistent efforts to lower the centre of gravity. First of all, even the engine's centre of gravity is already superbly low because – thanks to the V-180-degree construction – the heaviest components are to be found at the bottom of the engine. From the exhaust system to the cylinder heads with their camshafts, pistons and piston rods – all these components lie lower than they do in the Ford-Cosworth eight cylinder engine. Because of the design's symmetry about the crankshaft the Ferrari engine's centre of gravity turns up right in the centre of the crankshaft. The asymmetrical components like distributor head, fuel injection system (on top)

1 The frictional forces can only operate at road surface level. As in our theoretical case the centrifugal force would also be acting at road surface level there would be no 'lever arm' capable of causing changes in wheel loadings.

40

and exhaust (underneath) just about balance each other out. It is true that the Ford engine can, in terms of the crankshaft, be installed rather lower down because of course the whole engine block including its exhaust and cylinder heads juts out above it, but despite this there are still about five centimetres gain in the centre of gravity of the Ferrari car, solely thanks to the engine.

Of course the centre of gravity of the engine alone does not decided where the centre of gravity of the car will lie, as the engine is only about a quarter of the car's all up weight. The gearbox, radiator, oil cooler, battery and of course the monocoque are also important factors.

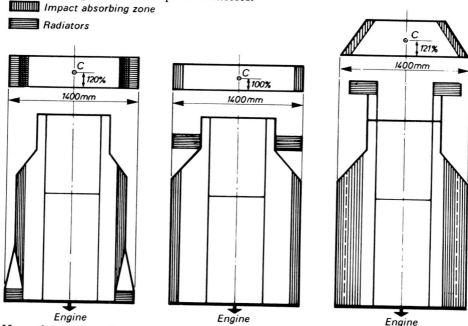

How the centre of gravity varies in different monocoque designs, given the same width and volume, and given the length. The basic advantage of the rectangle cross-section over the trapezium is clear from the geometry. Of the two rectangular designs shown, the left hand one is the scheme usually adopted in Formula I construction: a narrow body with side radiators. As these radiators do not extend the whole length of the vehicle, we are sacrificing volume which has to be compensated for by the increased height. The ideal design solution is that by Ferrari (centre diagram): The maximum width is exploited along virtually the entire length of car, which means a lower construction for the same given volume, and thus the lowest possible centre of gravity.

Centre of Gravity of the Chassis

To stay with the example of the Ferrari T 3 1 2 T. In the design of the monocoque there were several basic innovations, yet it differs – for the better – from its rivals. Let us start with the assumption that the width and cross-section area are fixed (the width by the rules of the sport that fix maximum width at 140 centimeters and the area by the fact that a certain minimum is necessary to accommodate the driver and the petrol – the length will be discussed later, but we assume identical wheelbases). Given this width and cross-section area, various different shapes are possible. From the viewpoint of the best centre of gravity, the optimum cross-sectional shape has to be a rectangle, as the diagram proves : with a trapezium, the centre of gravity is 21 per cent higher than with a rectangle. In this diagram as in practice an optical illusion suggests that the trapezium's centre of gravity is lower than the rectangle's – i.e. that the Brabham's or BRM's is lower than the Ferrari's : but in fact Ferrari is on the right track. To complete this solution, as rightly recognized by Ferrari, the radiators previously mounted on either side of the car now have to be installed next to the front wheel suspensions.

Thus Ferrari's design is also superior to the other cars sporting a rectangular cross-section, as Ferrari utilizes this cross-section over a much longer section of the body, while Lotus and the others utilize this optimum cross-section only at the very rear where the two external radiators are mounted (see the diagram). This means throwing away part of the cross-section, which has to be compensated for by a taller construction with consequent worsening of the centre of gravity's position. This difference is what gives the Ferrari its low, squat look. Naturally Lotus, Tyrrell and the others had their own strong reasons for selecting a narrow body with its protruding radiators : they rated the aerodynamic benefits of a narrow body higher than they did a low centre of gravity.

Up to this point we have assumed that all our cars have the same length. But this too is a variable : the longer the car, the shallower the rectangle or trapezium and hence the lower the centre of gravity. As there are good reasons for avoiding overhangs at either end, more length must also mean a longer wheelbase. The UOP Shadow opted for this design with very good results. But the disadvantages of long wheelbase cars are well-known : they handle badly on zigzag bends.

To sum up : we have so far dealt with the importance of load distribution, the height of the centre of gravity, the car body's rigidity and the suspension. There are still some criteria under which modern Formula I cars have to be regarded.

ALL UP WEIGHT

Although the maximum set by the rules is by no means low at 575 kilograms, only a few cars actually attain this ideal weight. From a design point of view it is difficult to do so, because as time passed more and more 'important' additions were made to the security regulations. It is naturally easier to keep to the limit with an eight-cylinder engine than with a twelve-cylinder engine : the weight difference can be put around 25 kg. The Ferrari exceeds the limit by about these 25 kg, so we have to shed as much weight as we can. With a power-to-weight ratio of 1.2 kg per horsepower it is obvious that every kilo counts.

WHEELBASE AND TRACK

Basically we can say that the smaller, narrower and shorter the car the easier it will handle and the better it will be suited to the new style race tracks (with more curves and more chicanes). A narrower *track* yields aerodynamic benefits because the wheels can be partly protected by bodywork in the rear or by wings at the front. The aerodynamic cross-section of the car as a whole is also reduced as a result. But a narrower track is a disavantage when taking corners at speed, as the load displacement to the outer wheels is greater than with cars with a wider track.

This brings us to the *wheelbase*. A shorter wheelbase makes for a handier car but, as already explained, it raises the centre of gravity. Thanks to its consistent exploitation of the available space the Ferrari can afford an extremely short wheelbase (only 250 centimetres) – a wheelbase of almost Formula II proportions despite the long twelve-cylinder engine.

PETROL TANKS

The petrol tank arrangement has a strong influence on a car's handling. Ideally the tanks should be distributed in such a manner round the centre of gravity that the car's weight distribution from front to rear and from right to left is always constant regardless of whether the tanks are full or almost empty. As there are at least three tanks in a Formula I car (and sometimes even five) a number of different tank arrangements are possible.

43

TOP SPEEDS

The aerodynamic aids, whose positive influence on the car's cornering has already been referred to, also affect a car's top speeds. The top speed depends on the shape and location of the wings, in addition to the engine's horsepower, the aerodynamic drag-coefficient and the car's cross-sectional area. All racing car designers are aiming at the same thing : as much down force as possible when cornering,[1] while sacrificing as little forward speed as possible : in other words a compromise has to be adopted. Verdicts on the best solution differ, and sometimes other design factors have to be taken into account : for example a Tyrrell-type nose would not be feasible on the Ferrari 12 T because then the radiators mounted just behind the front wheel-suspensions would not get enough draught. In the Brabham the radiators are an integral part of the nose, a design affording optimum cooling effect which means that the radiators themselves can be kept smaller than if they had been mounted on the car's sides. But the weight advantage of the Brabham idea is offset by the need for lengthy water pipes.

AIR BOXES

Air boxes are a chapter all of their own. They are what most of all gives each car its image. The basic job of the air box is to introduce air into the engine. The car's forward motion rams air into the box, the air is pushed into the inlet trumpets, and thus the engine is in a sense 'charged'. This supercharging effect is however very minor and does not arise until the forward speed exceeds 40 mph up to that speed the engine is inducting air faster than wind resistance is ramming it in. At 160 mph the ram force is 0.02 atmospheres, from which we can compute that the engine will gain about two per cent, or 10 horsepower, in power.

[1] On the straights the wings have more disadvantages than advantages. The disadvantages are these : the wings increase the aerodynamic cross section of the car and increase the wind resistance therefore. The wings divert the airflow according to the angle they are set at. If we resolve the resulting forces, into two components, the horizontal component is the wind resistance, the vertical one increases the down force which in turn increases the frictional resistance of the wheel bearings and tyres. The advantage is that the greater down force makes the car more stable and by increasing the rear wheel loading enhances acceleration performance. To keep the wings' negative factors within limits we resort to the design data obtained by aviation research. Car wings are designed like aeroplane wings, though mounted upside down as they are to create down force, not lift.

The more important part of the air box's job is to ensure that the engine is supplied with air at the ambient temperature, and the same amount to all cylinders. The box prevents the engine from inducting air already heated by brake discs, radiators, oil-coolers, exhaust manifolds and gearboxes. For instance, if the temperature of the inducted air is 20 degrees Centigrade above the ambient air temperature, the drop in engine efficiency will be four per cent, or twenty horsepower.

As against these two plus effects we must set one minus : the air box increases the car's wind resistance or drag, because it increases the aerodynamic cross-section by about three per cent.

In theory, therefore, the advantages of air boxes are not all that sensational. In trial runs however we have always found that on all Grand Prix tracks cars with air boxes are faster than those without.

* * *

This chapter will have shown that a very complicated interplay of factors decides whether, ultimately, a car has been well designed or not. Now a new set of interconnecting forces comes into effect to decide whether a particular car is tuned right for a particular day's racing. Behind the simple victory or defeat that we can watch on our TV screens, virtually without mention of any causes and effects, there are a host of practical concepts and details that have to be adjusted and brought into a mutual relationship with one another in all their manifold effects. Everybody has a say in this final compromise : the designer, the engineers, the mechanics, the team boss and the driver. So far we have been listening only to the theory : in the remaining chapters of this book we shall turn to the practice of the game.

Technical Data
of a Formula I Car taking the
Ferrari 312 T as an example

Monocoque with the engine as a partially stressed member and a transverse gearbox. Safety fuel tanks on either side in beam structure, two radiators behind front axle.

Dimensions and Weight

Overall length approximately 450 centimetres (depending on wing), overall width approximately 210 centimetres (depending on wheel rim width), overall height 130 centimetres, wheelbase 250 centimetres.

Track (equal front and rear) 115 to 160 centimetres (depending on wheel-rim width). All-up weight in road condition, but less petrol, 595 kilograms. Load distribution front to rear in ratio 40:60.

Engine

Engine 180-degree V 12, capacity 2,998 cc developing 495 horsepower (DIN-standard) at 11,800 rpm. Maximum permitted revolutions 12,400 rpm. Two overhead camshafts for each row of cylinders, four valves per cylinder. Sparking plugs positioned centrally between the valve inlets. Valve angle approximately 30 degrees. Two valve springs per valve. Crankshaft with four main bearings. Dry sump lubrication, oil capacity of eight litres, two oil-coolers. Main stream oil filter. Mechanical Lucas high-pressure fuel injection, throttle slide. Twelve-volt dry battery. Two radiators, total capacity ten litres of water, no fan.

Power Transmission

Twin disc dry clutch. Non synchromesh Ferrari five-speed gearbox in one unit with the differential (75 per cent locked) with joint oil cooling, by means of cooler in wing-mounting, and oil pump. Wheels driven by differential via homokinetic drive shafts. Gear ratios according to circuit.

Chassis and Suspension

Front axle : double triangular wishbones, inboard springs (coil springs, twin-tube liquid shock-absorbers), inboard anti-roll bar.

Back axle : two wishbones either side, a radius rod on either side, springs (as in front) and an anti-roll bar.

Steering : rack and pinion.

Brakes : internally aircooled disc brakes front and rear, brake callipers with four pistons, cooling by four air boxes. Independent braking systems front and rear using one master cylinder each (braking force distribution by means of balance bars).

Wheel rims : three sections with central joint. Front rims 10 inches by 13, rear rims 16, 17 or 18 inches by 13.

Tyres : 9.2/20.00 – 13 in the front, 16.2/26.0 – 13 in the rear, (or 16 psi front, 18 psi rear). Air pressure 1.1 atmospheres front, 1.2 atmospheres rear.

The Formula I Car's Components and How to Live with Them

The monocoque construction – it literally means 'made of one shell' – has now absolutely and without exception supplanted the tubular-frame construction for Formula I chassis. In the monocoque thin metal sheets and not individual tubes are the load-bearing components of the chassis; these metal sheets are usually rivetted to each other around corners. This construction has the same overall weight as the tubular frame design, but provides considerably more rigidity and allows the best possible exploitation of available space for the fuel tanks and safety devices. Being stronger, this design also gives better crash protection.

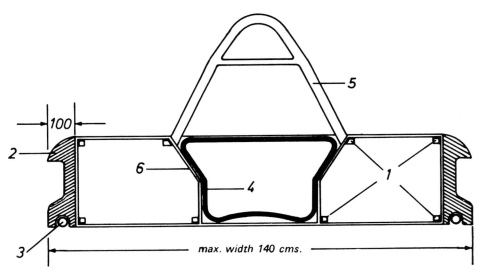

Schematic cross section of the monocoque taken at the driver's seat position. 1 : struts; 2 : impact absorbing zone; 3 : water hoses to radiators; 4 : seat bucket; 5 : roll bar; 6 : space for safety tanks.

Seen in cross-section, the car has the driver sitting between two beam structures which are sealed off front and rear by two load-bearing metal bulkheads on which are mounted the front wheel suspension and the engine at the rear. There is enough space inside each beam structure to accommodate the fuel tanks quite neatly, because they are just empty spaces not interlaced with any kind of tubular struts.

Normally this shell is assembled from individual aluminium sections, but at Ferrari they have their own distinctive approach to the monocoque. First they weld together a real frame from square steel rods, though without any transverse struts, and this provides a framework for the monocoque. And then the aluminium sheets are rivetted on to this frame – in other words to be precise the Ferrari monocoque is a combination of the tubular frame and the sheet metal shell techniques. The pros and cons are clear enough : it is more rigid and safer, but it weighs more and it costs more.

To the left and right the monocoque is clad with ten-centimetre thick impact-absorbing zones near the fuel tanks : these are foam-filled sandwich constructions that despite their light construction are able to disperse a lot of impact energy – the regulations relating to this are formulated very precisely but in view of their different possible interpretations they are not without their headaches for designers.

In the Ferrari the monocoque is sealed in front by a complicated cast-magnesium unit that has to serve many functions : in it are situated the two brake cylinders, the shock-absorbers and springs, the mounting points for the front suspension and the anti-roll bar. Other firms have adopted a rather less complex unit, using one or two aluminium plates to seal off the monocoque in front.

The rear bulkhead attaches the monocoque to the engine, which also has load-bearing functions. In many cars the Unibal universal joint[1] for the rear radius rods are also mounted on this bulkhead.

At any given weight the best monocoque is the one that bends and distorts least, because every chassis distortion will result in a deterioration in the car's road handling. For instance, the more rigid the car is the better it will respond to the anti-roll bars.

In all this striving for rigidity one thing becomes clear – that the centre

[1] The Unibal universal joint in every Formula car has to be free of play and need no servicing. It transmits forces from suspension components, that are naturally moving, into the bodywork. As these motions are complicated and random the ball-joint has to be able to move freely in every direction, at least to a certain extent.

section of the monocoque, where the driver sits, will be the sore point. This aperture has to be kept as small as possible. That is why the driver's leg room is also covered in. A cross-member beneath the instrument panel (i.e., over the driver's knees) keeps the two box sections apart. You just cannot have too much rigidity : as the roll bar is supported both front and rear by struts, this also lends something to the car's overall rigidity. Moreover simple tubular constructions help stiffen the junction of motor and gearbox to the monocoque.

The rules lay down a maximum width, and virtually every designer exploits this to the limit, but there are still extraordinary differences in the shape of one monocoque from another. These differences are partly the product of design factors (radiators, oil-cooler, the length of the car) which of themselves render an optimum solution of the centre-of-gravity equation impossible. The earlier tendency to keep the body narrow has long been superseded : to keep that centre of gravity as low as possible designers now build their cars as flat and broad as possible and dispense with the anyway highly debatable aerodynamic advantages of a narrow body.

A further aspect in monocoque design is the positioning of the fuel tanks with regard to the car's centre of gravity. Experience has shown that the shift in the centre of gravity when the tanks are more or less full has a big influence on the way a car handles. So we have to try to position the tanks so that the car's centre of gravity is as independent as possible of the petrol quantity remaining at any given moment. This is the only way of ensuring that the ideal road handling attained in test drives will obtain throughout an entire Grand Prix distance.

MY WORKPLACE

My workplace in this car is naturally cramped, but I sit comfortably and relaxed and I can reach all the controls without impossible contortions and I have a good view of all the instruments. It is a good thing when my team mates and I are of the same build, so we can swap cars without having to make any kind of adjustments. The bucket seat is adjusted to fit the driver once and for all – and obviously a Hans-Joachim Stuck would not find enough room in a Ferrari marked with the Number 11.

I am very fussy about the little things that matter in my workplace. The pedals have to be positioned just right, and so do the footrests, the steering wheel and gear lever as otherwise I just cannot concentrate on driving. The driver cannot afford to be irritated by little details. One example of how things can still go wrong however hard you try is this: during my victory in the Grand Prix at Monaco in 1975 there was a horse-hair that gave me misery – it stuck out of the knee-padding on the left and it was so sharp that it bored right through my overalls and jabbed me every time I took a right hand corner. There is absolutely nothing you can do to stop something like that: when you are fastened into your seat you cannot even reach your knee even if you have time to do so – which you do not – and your thick gloves would get in the way anyway.

The most dominant instrument is the rev counter. Its scale goes from 4,000 to 14,000 revs per minute. The needle climbs smoothly, in other words it does not skip and bounce like the rev counters in most sports cars. Nor does our rev counter waver to and fro, as it takes no notice of the rapid rev changes or of the powerful vibrations transmitted by the rigidly mounted engine to the entire car.

In the Ferrari there is no tell-tale (a pointer that is dragged round by the rev counter needle to the highest rev count reading and left there to betray your driving sins). But we do have an electronic rev limiter which can be pre-set by a small screw to operate at any desired reading: if you take the engine up to this pre-set limit it will begin missing slightly, as – initially – individual spark impulses are cut out; in each case the effect will just be sufficient to retain the car's speed, a point of particular importance when taking curves with the engine nearing this pre-set limit, as this is the only way to ensure continued control of the car. Revolution limiters that briefly cut out the ignition current altogether when the rev limit is reached and bring it down by 200 rpm have proved a failure, as the sudden loss of engine power can cause tricky situations. In my own car the device is set to operate at 12,400 or 12,500 rpm. Of course I try not to reach this limit, as I lose power when the spark impulses are cut – power I could have made good use of if I had changed gear at the right moment. Just in case, there is a tumbler switch located in the cockpit to override the rev limiter: because for instance there may be different wind conditions during a race from those that prevailed during the last practice session with the result that, although the car is unchanged you may be running at 200 or 300 rpm more in fifth gear. This may happen when you are in somebody else's slipstream on long straights too. If that happens you do not just stand back while your opponents pull ahead, but override the rev limiter so as to get the benefit of the extra ten miles an hour or so at the end of the range. The engine will just about take it. Besides, the override switch is also necessary because the electronic rev limiter is a delicate contraption that sometimes goes haywire and starts cutting back at 10,000 rpm or even lower.

The instruments showing petrol pressure in the injection system and the engine's oil pressure are combined in one instrument to the right of the rev counter. For better distinction between them the petrol indicator is white, the oil indicator red. The petrol pressure scale goes from 4 to 14 kilograms per square centimetre (the normal value is twelve). What is interesting is that the cars have two petrol pumps, a mechanical one driven by the engine and an electrical one powered by the car's electrical circuit. There are two reasons for this : we want to avoid petrol continuing to be pumped by the electrical pump if the engine stops, for instance after a crash. Thus the electrical pump may only be operated by a spring loaded switch during the starting procedure, to provide the petrol pressure necessary for the injection system. After the engine starts the electrical pump is switched off as the start switch is released, and the mechanical pump takes over the fuel delivery, powered by the engine itself. This can give headaches if the engine revs fall below 4,000 rpm as the mechanical pump is then no longer able to provide enough petrol pressure. Low revs like these may result if the car goes into a spin, or in a wet race because we tend to drive at lower revs then to make the car more docile. The only thing to do then is to switch in the electrical petrol pump again to stop the engine dying on you.

A further reason for the presence of two petrol pumps is the high electricity consumption of the electrical pump : we do not want to inflict this load on the car's electric system and its anyway very diminutive battery more than very briefly.

The oil pressure indicator registers from nil to 15 kilograms per square centimetre. Once the oil is at the right temperature and the car is being raced the indicator will waver between 8 and 9. When ticking over or running at low revs the needle will fall to 2 kilograms per square centimetre. As the oil pressure is also dependent on the oil temperature, the pressure may well drop on a hot racing day by one or two units on account of the reduced viscosity.

A further combined instrument indicates the oil and water temperature (on the left of the rev. counter). The red needle for the oil and the white needle for the water pivot on the same centre, so they cover the same scale, which runs from 40 to 130 degrees Centigrade. As the water cooling system is under pressure water temperatures up to 110 degrees are possible without the water boiling. Under normal conditions the water temperature is around 95 degrees. The oil temperature must not exceed 120 degrees. I did hit record temperatures – I would prefer not to reveal just how high they went – at Monza in 1974 when a water hose coupling worked loose. Shortly after that the engine died. As the Ferrari engine is rather sensitive to heat – more about that in the chapter

The dotted line shows the outline of the monocoque. With the bodywork removed it is possible to see how the leg room between the two box sections is covered by stiffeners.

The dream of fans and racing drivers alike — to sit at the controls of the Ferrari 312 T. The only warning light, positioned between rev counter and oil pressure indicator, will flash red if the oil pressure drops too low. The little instrument visible bottom right beyond the edge of the bucket seat shows whether the fire extinguisher under the driver's knees is full enough. The really sharp-eyed observer will detect under the left spoke of the steering wheel the die-stamped chassis number 022: in this car I won the Daily Express trophy against Fittipaldi at Silverstone.

The emergency air-supply bottle is connected to the helmet by a fireproof hose. The airpipe projecting to the left rear of the helmet continues inside it, and ends just in front of the driver's mouth.

The main electrical switch is normally manually operated. It is on the right, on a wing support, near the battery so as to minimize the cable length. The cylinder visible beneath the switch contains an explosive pellet which will throw the switch if the car's emergency switch is operated.

The emergency air-supply bottle for crash survival is strapped to a cross strut of the roll bar. The air-pipe hanging down in this picture is connected to a tube in the driver's crash-helmet. The two arrows point to the jets from which fire-extinguishing halon gas is sprayed round the driver.

The six point seat belt.

It is not possible to fasten the seat belt without the help of mechanics – the driver is too cramped.

on engines – our attention to the thermometer on hot days is particularly close.

The switches in the Ferrari cockpit are these : rocker switch for rear light (in rain or fog), rocker switch for rev limiter override – both to the right of the pressure indicator; a push button starter, a press button switch for the electrical petrol pump – both to the left of the thermometer. There too is a switch (with a red safety cover) that may save our lives in an emergency. When it is operated, several things happen simultaneously : the main fire extinguisher is switched on by an explosive pellet, spraying the entire cockpit, the driver and the fuel tanks with halon gas; the engine's fire extinguisher is operated, the driver's emergency air supply bottle is opened by an explosive pellet, delivering air via a pipeline to his crash helmet, and to a pipe ending right in front of his mouth; and another explosive pellet throws the main battery switch to the off position.

Most prominent of all is the 'kill switch' attached to the right spoke of the steering wheel. It has to be that close at hand, in case the accelerator jams wide open in which case we can then kill the ignition immediately. A raised leather ring round the centre of the steering wheel prevents us from knocking the switch to off by accident. The 'off' position is clearly marked so that even if the wheel is turned right round it is impossible to make a mistake.

Fastening ourselves into a Formula I car is a big business, because our six point seat belts are so complicated that they cannot be buckled up by a driver by himself. A simple four-point seat belt, like trouser-braces, would not be adequate, as the driver's body is so rear-inclined that in a head-on crash he would just slip down through the waist belt. This has to be prevented by the addition of two extra belt fastening points beneath the seat. From these two belt segments are passed, initially together between the legs and then parting across the thighs to go through a strap eyelet on the waist belt to meet at the belt release which has to lie dead centre in the abdomen. This is a rotating release : when the centre lever is twisted five belt segments drop loosely out of the buckle. Tests were made with a punch-release, but these failed as the abdomen yields too much under pressure to open such a buckle every time.

The cockpit is so cramped that for a driver to buckle himself in would be quite out of the question. It always takes two mechanics to do it, one standing on each side of the car and making the necessary belt adjustments.

If we are once forced to stop somewhere along the track to check something or repair a minor fault – which means we have to unbuckle ourselves – then we have to drive slowly back to the pits afterwards to be buckled in again. To fail to do this would be the worst possible disregard for elementary safety precautions.

Under no circumstances must the belt be so tight that it creates any pressure points or even interferes with the blood circulation to the legs causing them consequently to go numb or fall asleep.

I myself can only adjust the length of the two belt segments passing over my shoulders. By tightening or loosening the two rapid tensioning devices on them I can adjust the entire tension so that the belt-web, the seat and I myself as driver all fit snugly together.

Lest anybody should maintain that Formula I cars sound Spartan: we even have an integrated headrest, though it is not designed to lean back on so much as to catch the head and heavy safety helmet in the event of a rear-end collision to prevent spinal injuries. In my view the other Formula cars pay too little attention to such simple and cheap safety precautions.

The Driver's Personal Equipment

The importance of the right dress is self-evident: underwear and overalls are made of fire resistant material, and the clothes also naturally have to overlap. For instance the gloves must be long enough to overlap the overall sleeves by six inches. The mask has to reach right up to the eyes, and be tucked into the overalls at the bottom. The idea is to offer the flames as little human surface as possible in a fire.

More recently the visors have been manufactured from 3 millimetre Perspex to prevent face and eye injuries from flying stones. To protect their hearing all racing drivers plug their ears with Oropax wax. These ear plugs primarily cut out the high frequency sounds like engine noise while still allowing the drivers to converse reasonably well with other people. Now an American firm has brought out something new: a kind of soft plastic substance that is first compressed in your hands and then plugged into your ear. It thereupon expands slowly again and is particularly 'soundproof'.

THE ENGINE

Logically enough all engines used in Formula I are close to the maximum size of 3,000 cc. Further features common to all the engines are their aluminium construction, their use of mechanical fuel injection systems and four valves per cylinder. The fuel intake is regulated in all the engines by a throttle-slide, which has one advantage over the butterfly-type throttle valve, namely that it opens up the entire intake cross-section when the throttle is wide open; but it can cause problems too, as foreign objects may become lodged between the slide and the slide housing, thus jamming the slide. The valves are operated by cams acting directly on the valve shafts. The modern trend inclines increasingly to ever smaller valve angles.

Basic pros and cons need only be briefly mentioned. In theory a twelve-cylinder engine ought to be more efficient, but it also has to make up for the added weight and fuel consumption. Assuming an average power-to-weight ratio of 1.2 kilograms per horsepower in a Formula I car, a 24 kilogram heavier engine would have to develop 20 more horsepower to give the same ratio – not to mention the extra petrol consumption. Even if two cars of different all-up weights have the same power-to-weight ratio, the lighter car will always have the edge over the other as all its components, particularly the tyres, will be under correspondingly less strain.

I am probably the only driver who has had dealings with three engines in my career – the Ford Cosworth V8, the BRM and the Ferrari. Most of all I prefer the Ferrari, not just because of its power but because of the broad band of usable revs. From 4,000 to 12,300 rpm the engine runs very sweetly and already has a lot of pulling power at only 4,000 rpm. You may think that a Grand Prix car does not have much driving to do at these engine revs, but you would not be entirely right : at Monte Carlo and on other courses too there are hairpin bends which you could only take with a Cosworth V8 engine by dropping into bottom gear, because the Ford engine only begins to run smoothly and develop power over and above 6,000 rpm. Accelerating away from these tight corners it then often is not easy to give the engine exactly the right amount of throttle to avoid going into a slide and losing the car's smooth performance. With the Ferrari engine we can get out of situations like this much easier and faster : we just keep in second gear – thus avoiding two gear-changes – and accelerate again after the curve with much more feeling for the road, with more continuity and with less slip; and after that we can rev the engine without any loss of power or pulling strength right up to the maximum revs again.

It may sound incredible but it is the truth : we can drive our Ferrari just like a Volkswagen. We just let in the clutch with the engine merely idling, and then accelerate away without the slightest jerk. In wet races where we can only release the power to the wheels bit by bit because of the reduced tyre grip this is particularly important and I find it more reliable too than an engine that begins to cough under 6,000 revs and backfires and only shows its real fangs at higher revs than that. In fact the Ford Cosworth engine has something of the character of a two-stroke engine, because that too only begins to pull after

Theoretically Possible Engines of 3,000 cc

Number of cylinders	Cubic capacity of each cylinder in cc	Bore (centimetres)	Stroke (centimetres)	Each piston face area (square centimetres)	Total piston face area (square centimetres)	Revs per minute assuming average piston speed 21.5 metres per second	Engine's HP rating at average pressure of 12.5 kilos per sq cm
4	750	11.09	7.76	96.59	386.36	8,311	346.3
6	500	9.68	6.78	73.59	441.54	9,513	396.4
8	375	8.80	6.16	60.82	486.56	10,470	436.2
12	250	7.68	5.38	46.32	555.84	11,988	499.5

This table shows the data of four theoretically possible three-litre engines with different numbers of cylinders. For all the engines we assume a stroke to bore ratio of 0.7 and an average piston velocity of 21.5 metres per second (the usual Formula I specifications). We see that the engine with most cylinders naturally has the smallest area per individual piston face but also the largest total acting surface. As the power transmitted by the pistons via the piston rods to the crankshaft is dependent not only on the combustion force but also on the surface on which that force acts the first advantage of such an engine with a large number of cylinders becomes obvious. Another factor in favour of the twelve-cylinder engine is that given equal average piston speed it will rev. faster than the eight-cylinder engine: and as the revolutions are one factor governing an engine's performance the advantage is equally obvious. In the last column of the table are the horsepower ratings calculated for these four engines using the performance formula for four-stroke engines.

This big theoretical performance advantage of the twelve-cylinder engine over the other engines is in practice strongly offset – in particular by the increased internal friction and by the fact that the average pressure assumed in this calculation (12.5 kilograms per square centimetre) is exceeded in engines with a smaller number of cylinders (because there is an improved fuel and air mixture in the engines running at lower revs.). In practice therefore the twelve-cylinder is no more than about 7 to 10 per cent more powerful than the eight-cylinder.

it reaches a certain rpm. And the three engines also have very distinctive sounds : the Ferrari sound is even more diabolic than the roar of the BRM, compared to which the Ford engine sounds quite tame. The more the cylinders and the higher the revs, the worse the noise; the noise is also affected by the camshaft timing and the relationship of intake and exhaust timings.

The Ferrari engine is not a horizontally opposed one but a V-engine aligned at 180 degrees. The rods of two opposing pistons are connected to one common crankshaft offset. This results in an advantage over the horizontally opposed design in which two opposing pistons are always acting against each other, namely that the air in the crankshaft casing is merely pushed backwards and forwards; this leads to less wasteful work than in the horizontally opposed form in which the opposing pistons are constantly having to compress and expand this air cushion beneath them.

One particular problem in the Ferrari engine is how to retain its full performance over long distances. The loss of performance as between new and overhauled engines is minimal – only some 5 horsepower – but any given engine driven over the full Grand Prix distance will lose about 20 horsepower. It is an unusual effect, as most racing engines do not even attain their best performance until they have been run in for a while. The consequence of this special Ferrari handicap is that after every practice session we always install a new engine so that we do not start off on the wrong foot by throwing away valuable performance. We believe that the technical reason for this weakness lies in the engine's poor water jacket design which results in the cylinders and cylinder head distorting under high oil and water temperatures. This results in the first case in compression leakage past the piston rings, while in the second case the valve seatings distort preventing the valves from closing properly which in turn results in them overheating. Hot valves do not enhance performance, naturally, because they will in turn heat up the petrol-air mixture.[1] Even on the test rigs, our engineers have noticed that there is a considerable loss of performance at oil and water temperatures at which other engines are only just beginning to loosen up. For this reason we have recently been paying extra attention to the piston rings; we have picked up a few extra horsepower again and managed to lessen this loss of performance over long distances.

At the beginning of the 1976 season the average performance of a new Ferrari engine was rated at 495 horsepower (at 11,800 rpm). This gave us an estimated

---

[1] It is the mass and not the volume of the inducted air that counts. Greater weight means more oxygen which means more power. As the air becomes hotter, however, so it becomes lighter.

edge of 25 horsepower over most of our rivals. It sounds a lot, but we cannot make full use of it because of the engine's higher weight and increased petrol consumption. What this in practice means is that we have to pay close attention to fuel consumption : if we have to line up at the start with about $4\frac{1}{2}$ gallons more petrol than the other competitors, that adds another 22.5 kilograms to our all-up weight. So during the practice we try to adjust the petrol-air mixture until it is as lean as possible – which again does not help our engine's performance much because engines are known to run best on a slightly enriched mixture. If we take this process too far, we will find out that the mixture is too weak when the engine begins missing between 7,000 and 9,000 revs. But Ferrari have built their own modification to the Lucas injection system to enable us to enrich the mixture again just for this rpm range.

As with every fast-rotating twelve-cylinder engine there was one other big problem to be solved : because the crankshaft has to be long it is vulnerable to torsional vibration. It took a long period of engine damage caused by crankshaft breakage before people began to apply themselves to the vibrations in this crankshaft system. First they reduced the mass (weight) of every component of the vibrational system – pistons, piston rods, crankshaft and flywheel with clutch. None of these changes took the problem much further. It was only when they set about taking the entire flywheel and clutch assembly right out of the vibrating system that they found the answer. In today's adaptation the flywheel is no longer rigidly bolted to the crankshaft but attached to it by a rubber element that gives it a limited amount of rotational freedom from the crankshaft. When this rubber element and all the rotating masses have been properly calculated the flywheel will simultaneously act as a damper on the torsional vibrations. And this in turn has also left its imprint on the new crankshaft's shape : it now looks quite delicate, and it has only four main bearings.

The Ferrari engineers undertook particularly detailed research into the design of the cylinder head and combustion chamber shape. They took the risk of departing from big valves; since then the small valve angle (about 30 degrees) has become something of a standard for new racing engine designs. The main advantages of the small valve angle lie in the better combustion chamber shape (there is no need for a convex piston face) and straighter air passages – these more than offset the handicap of the smaller valve angle.

The quality of this engine design is evident for example from the sparking plugs. The plugs do not oil up or cause any other problems either while the engine is warming up or during its normal running. In all the time I have been dealing with Ferrari engines I have never yet had to use warm-up spark plugs or change them. I might add that that is a good thing too, because to change even individual sparking plugs it is necessary to dismantle large parts of the engine.

Overall we can sum up the qualities of the Ferrari engine like this : its higher horsepower is probably offset almost entirely by its greater weight and petrol consumption, so that its net remaining advantages are these :

○ the broad band of usable revs.
○ the ultra-low engine centre of gravity which of course has a powerful beneficial effect on the centre of gravity of the car as a whole.
○ the engine's rigidity.

To take extra care and to take account of the loss of performance that was mentioned earlier there is a practice engine and a proper racing engine for each race. The practice engine is assembled from components like pistons, piston rods, crankshaft and valves that have already several hours' running behind them. Every such component is carefully logged so we can determine instantly how old it is. For the actual race engine we use virtually only new components in order to obviate any breakdowns from metal fatigue as far as possible.

We Ferrari men belong body and soul to our engines – we devote every ounce of our energy and emotions to these artefacts of aluminium, magnesium and steel. And in recent years our affection has been rewarded by loyalty : for a Ferrari engine to break down has now become only a sensational exception.

I am no less affectionate than the others : I call each new engine I get 'mio nuovo figlio' – my new son. I do not really care much for technology, but I always end up feeling something like a love-affair for my engine : for instance if I am careless and crash the gears I often feel like driving straight back to the pits and chucking up the whole game, I am so furious with myself.

It is difficult to state exactly a rev maximum that would completely write off the engine because of for instance the valves clashing with each other or hitting the pistons. In theory this should have happened at about 12,800 rpm but there was one case when by error I let the engine race on to 13,500 rpm without damaging it in any way.

The engine's main sign of life is a red lamp on the dashboard : it does not out when the engine finally dies, but comes on. The electrical contact operat this lamp is linked to the oil pressure. If the pressure drops below 4 kilogram per square centimetre, the lamp lights – by which time the engine usually mangled itself anyway because somewhere a big hole has app revealing the engine's innards. Not that the news has to come as bluntly a during a race your heart will drop to your driving boots even if your familiar note just changes suddenly or you see a plume of smoke trailing behind you in your driving mirror. You run your eye over all the instruments : if there's nothing out of the ordinary there, I try to get a picture of the damage as fast as possible because my first priority is to pass the finishing line at all costs and I can still do that even if my car has developed trouble during the race.

One example of a relatively harmless defect is if an exhaust pipe splits or I lose one of my four conically shaped exhaust tailpipes. I can diagnose that when the next straight comes if not earlier, because the engine will suddenly lose power and make about 300 rpm less. But that will not cause any further consequential damage.

What is less pleasant is if a valve spring breaks. For safety reasons every valve in this engine has two springs, so there are 96 all told. If a spring breaks the engine will only behave properly up to a certain rpm and above that it loses power. The breakage of an outer spring is worse than an inner spring because the outer one is the stronger and most of the spring's shutting power depends n it. Whichever of the two, if a valve spring breaks in a race you have got to 've on very sedately because you run the risk of writing off the whole engine. practice you would drive straight back to the pits in such an event and the engine changed.

see a stream of oil spraying out behind you – what then? You can see it in your mirror, but it may indicate only a harmless defect, for instance ing from a leak onto the hot exhaust. But if the oil is coming from the hen that spells out sudden death for it because it means that it is t for some reason, and we know only too well it will not take that

sty sight is short puffs of oil smoke, growing longer after a while. ing the over-run and changing gear and they show that a piston l or a piston has been damaged. This allows engine oil to get on chamber during the over-run, and when you then put your it burns and causes the oil smoke plume. But all such reflections late if at the same time as the engine note changes the oil ngine suddenly chokes to a stop with a broken piston ring pouring from it.

r
m
m
go
ting
mes
has
eared
that :
ngine's

ng Ferrari I have admired the precision and deft-
old Ferrari 312 B 3's gearbox was already con-

63

siderably easier in this respect than the Hewland gearbox of its competitors, but in the new 312 T Ferrari have surpassed themselves. In this Ferrari five-speed gearbox the pinion shaft and the main drive shaft lie *transverse* to the car's direction of travel (hence the letter T in the car's model number); this is for reasons of space. So the gears lie in the direction of travel. This gearbox's space saving design already takes into account that in the near future the present rear wheel suspension may be replaced by a De-Dion rear axle, for whose cross connection there must obviously be enough room available. In any case this new gear box is a technological marvel designed and built at staggering cost – putting the Ferrari head and shoulders above all the Formula cars.

Every gearbox is carefully run in during trials and then closely scrutinized to ensure that the working surfaces of the gear teeth and the bearings are perfect. After that the box is reassembled and installed in the actual race car. This systematic work pays in the long run, because it brings freedom from gearbox damage.

Like all Formula gearboxes this one is non-synchromesh, which means that I can change up like lightning without declutching, but I have to double-declutch and touch the accelerator when changing down.

You can effect every gear change with just two fingers. The little gear lever is held in a gate with three levels, which is also something unusual on Formula racing. Thanks to this gate we enjoy two refinements designed to avoid damaging the engine and gearbox by selecting the wrong gears. Firstly, reverse can only be engaged if the proper release catch is first lifted; this prevents us from snarling the reverse gear. Secondly a slide mechanism built into this gate stops us accidently selecting first gear when we change down from fourth to third. (The gear layout is as in the BMW five-speed gearbox : reverse and first are in one level, second and third in another and fourth and fifth in another). Only after second gear has been engaged is the slot for the lever to enter first gear opened. It is a sensible arrangement that prevents over-revving through faulty gear selection when changing down, and it avoids possible spin caused by the over-brutal brake effect of the driving wheels at the instant the clutch is let in again.

Gear ratios

I make a point of selecting gear ratios so that in fifth gear I will just reach maximum revs (12,300 rpm) at the end of the longest straight on whichever track it is. This holds true for a race in which I can calculate on the basis of having the inside position – or because the track is particularly to my liking – I can calculate on getting ahead of the field so I can settle down to my own optimum laps. Things will be different if I expect to be slipstreaming (for example at Zeltweg) or if the race meeting is on a very gusty day. In these cases I would have the fifth gear about 250 to 300 rpm longer, about 2.5 per cent, so as not to run the risk of over-revving the engine if I get into the slipstream of others or find a strong tail wind.

We can see how vital it is for the individual gears to be correctly selected from the fact that no two Grand Prix tracks call for the same optimum transmission gearing. To win seconds on individual curves by means of better gearing I often have the appropriate ratios changed by 200 rpm upwards or downwards during the trials which may not make my mechanics at all happy with me, as most of them just cannot understand how such footling adjustments can possibly bring about any advantage.

The individual gears are allocated according to the track's various bends in such a manner that when I accelerate out of a bend with a particular gear I just reach the maximum revs. For instance, if on the entire track there is no fourth-gear curve, then I choose the fourth gear transmitted in such a way that the rev-jump from third to fourth gear is bigger than the jump from fourth to fifth – and in this way I obtain maximum acceleration on the straights. If there is a very important fourth-gear curve (I say important, because on very fast curves you will lose or gain more time than on the slow ones) then I deliberately suit the fourth gear to that curve regardless of the ideal relationship between third and fifth as far as acceleration is concerned.

In this way we work out our own gear ratios on the basis of the track's most important bends. Obviously this only works out as easy as it sounds on really simple tracks. On long tracks like the Nürburgring with a multiplicity of different curves and bends you can only go for a compromise, which is strongly dependent on the driver's own feelings. If a gear ratio is not quite right for a particular bend because it is too long for example (your revs are too low) then you will have no chance against a competitor who has selected the right ratio for this bend : when you both accelerate out of it, he will pull smoothly away from you. In this way it is possible for two cars to differ on different parts of the track although both may have the same lap times.

The actual changing of ratios in the Ferrari gearbox is pretty difficult – at any rate more difficult than in the Hewland gearbox used by all the other Formula I cars. In the Hewland all that is necessary to get at the gear shafts is to unscrew the rear gearbox cover. But as these shafts in the new Ferrari gearbox lie

Engine cooling is performed by altogether four radiators.
Both the two water radiators and the two oil coolers are integral parts
of the bodywork; the water radiators are mounted externally to right and left of
the driver's feet. The air stream flows beneath the front nose and beneath the
upper and lower wishbones into these radiators. The exit ports for this cooling-
air stream (this picture) are on either side of the driver's knees. This stream of
hot air has to be deflected so that it cannot impinge on the oil coolers to the
rear. The water radiators are linked to the engine by four aluminium tubes. The
upper tubes run past the driver's left and right shoulders, the return tubes
are freely suspended under the car's body in a channel in the impact absorbent
zone. The car's cooling system capacity is 10 litres of water.

The two oil coolers lie to right and left of the engine almost parallel to the
direction of travel, and are built in parts of the bodywork. This picture shows
the right oil cooler (after the bodywork is removed), in front of which can be
seen the dry sump lubrication's oil reservoir, with a transparent pipe (arrow)
enabling us to read off the oil level. Total oil: 8 litres. In front of this reservoir
(in terms of the direction of travel) can be seen the (as yet uncoupled) return
tube of the water cooling system and the channel provided for it underneath the
impact absorbent zone.

*An impressive view of a magnificent Formula I power plant: the stable housing
500 Ferrari horses. On top of and in the centre of the engine is the horizontal
oil filter, left and in front of it the distributor head, and from the injection
tubes visible just to its right we can see where the pump is. And what we cannot
see: deep down below are 48 valves and 96 valve springs!*

*View of the Ferrari engine's right cylinder block. There are wire-mesh masks
over the short air intake trumpets to prevent them from sucking in foreign bodies.
We can see from the narrowness of the cylinder head cover that the camshafts
lie quite close together, so the valve angle is a small one. The exhaust pipes are
masterpieces of tube-bending. Note one of the main fastening bolts holding the
engine to the cockpit (1) and the cooling system connections (2).*

View of the Ferrari engine seen from the monocoque connection end. Note the exceptionally shallow design, and the low centre of gravity. The arrows show the main fastening points for the monocoque. Above the two upper points can be seen the cooling system outlets (sealed with sticky tape). Half way down each side can be seen the lugs for the Unibal universal joint.

Gearbox view of the Ferrari engine with flywheel and clutch. The exhaust pipes of three cylinders on the same ignition timing are first brought together (as in the picture) then joined into one tail pipe further along the system (not photographed), so that there are four such tail pipes altogether. (The individual tubes leading to the lower pair of tail pipes are not visible in this photograph.) Behind the cover plate (1) are the two camshafts of the left cylinder block; the upper camshaft on the right cylinder block operates the worm gear driving the rev counter (2).

A safety catch has to be lifted in order to select reverse gear. The cast metal gear-lever gate is a practical example of the Ferrari's quality and finish. (Bodywork removed for the purpose of this photograph.) Also visible on this picture: the thick aluminium tube (light coloured) for the water cooling system running along the cockpit edge. Above it the flexible drive of the rev counter and an armoured cable.

The gearbox separated from the engine. The thin tubes take the brake fluid pressure to the two four-piston brake callipers directly mounted on the gearbox and acting on the internally air-cooled brake discs outside the gearbox.

The oil cooler for the gearbox-
differential system is built into the wing
support, open to the airstream to the
necessary extent in front. The oil flow
through the aluminium cooler is from
bottom to top, in order to carry
unwanted air out of the system. All the
tube connections are borrowed from
aircraft manufacture, and are made
of magnesium metal. Directly in front
of the support is the battery. Also visible
on this picture: the rear internally air-
cooled brake discs. To improve their
cooling there were two big air boxes,
naturally open to the front, which gulp
in air and direct it into the centre of
the brake discs. Also clearly visible here
are upper and low wishbones and the
tail lamp above the oil cooler. This
lamp has to be switched on in poor
visibility like rain or fog.

A vivid picture of the compactness of the
new Ferrari gearbox. We can see the left
brake callipers and the brake disc, with its
four spiral furrows for better brake-dust
ejection. Arrowed are the sockets for the
lower wishbone's universal joints.

crosswise, the entire right wheel suspension has to be dismantled: this is the only way to get at the bolts fastening the gear box cover. Compared with the Hewland, this involves an extra two hours' labour for one gear change during which the drive shaft and the entire wheel suspension has to be dismantled and reassembled.

The Differential

In all modern Formula cars the differential is designed as an automatic function limited-slip differential. The slip can be varied by inserting or removing shims or by tightening them, and it has a beneficial effect on the car's handling. What we want to achieve is this: we have to limit the amount that one wheel can spin when we drive off or hit a patch of road with unequal grip; the same thing can happen if the wheel on one side momentarily leaves the ground. Secondly: if we are taking a corner fast and need a lot of power for it, the inside driving wheel will only have a greatly diminished wheel loading because of the centrifugal forces, which means that it cannot transmit as much drive force to the road. Without the automatic limited-slip differential this wheel would then spin and as a result the outer wheel would not impart much driving force either as in a normal differential the flow of power normally takes the line of least resistance, in other words it would rush to the spinning wheel. Without the slip-limiter it would not even be possible to retain the same speed during the curve, not to speak of actually accelerating out of it.

When the car is moving fast across a road surface of irregular grip the slip-limiter helps to stabilize it, which is particularly important on a wet surface. There have even been experiments with completely blocked differentials, and they worked out better than might have been thought; but there are problems if you put your foot down when coming out of the curve, as the front of the car is then levered too much to the outside. In practice a 75 per cent limitation has been shown to work best.

The higher this limitation factor and the more we rely on it (because of numerous bends) the more the shims are subjected to friction and the greater the heat they generate. This is why the gearbox/differential assembly has its own oil flow and oil-cooler system built vertically into the wing mounting. A

Waiting for the flag (with bodywork removed).
Centre-spread: 'My finest race', Monaco 1975.
Ferrari's test track at Fiorano: It's Regazzoni's number, but I'm at the wheel.

72

small oil pump is built permanently into the gearbox. There are two hose couplings on the gear-box, by means of which it is linked to the oil-cooler. There is no instrument provided for the rear-axle temperature (it would only distract you in a race and there is nothing you can do about it anyway); one is installed during practice temporarily to enable us to fix the right size for the oil cooler. The oil temperature ought not to exceed 120 degrees.

TYRES

Before you read this section I would like to remind you of the basic principles stated at the beginning of the book, as this will help to explain the rather complicated subject of tyres.

If on some tracks we can no longer clip seconds off the record laps of recent years this is a result of the changed tyre situation. The earlier practice was to experiment a lot with different rubber compounds and tyre designs, while today there are by and large only two different compounds from one and the same tyre firm, namely Goodyear. I personally was happier with the earlier situation because I was able to gain an edge over my competitors on the basis of numerous trial runs and the close study of the materials involved : I just worked that little bit harder than the rest. But now Firestone has abandoned the game for economy reasons, and Goodyear has drastically reduced their product range. Although this has led to a degree of standardization, the subject of tyres still seems inexhaustible.

Demands

The tyres have to size up to a number of variables : the track surface, its cleanliness, road surface temperature, ambient temperature, the car's all up weight and load distribution, the adjustment of the car's aerodynamic aids. While fully aware of the complex nature of these factors and their relationships every driver is still in a position to get the very best out of the tyres although they are the same tyres for all the competitors. There is always a man from the tyre firm on hand to help the drivers, and he naturally knows best about the design and potential of each tyre.

Design

All racing tyres are cross-ply tyres. Tyres of radial design have not so far been used in racing : to obtain a clear picture as to their suitability for racing it would take an enormous outlay in development costs.

Conforming to this crossply design, the individual layers of the carcass are arranged diagonally to the direction of travel. Only tubeless tyres are used in Formula I, firstly because of the reduced weight and secondly because of the problems that assembling such wide tyres with inner tubes would cause. As the rim diameter front and rear is equal but the tyres themselves are of vastly different diameter it is obvious that the sidewalls of the front tyres are very low. This results in a tyre of great lateral stability, as it cannot be easily deformed with respect to the rim. This tyre rigidity on the front axle, where the steering wheels are, makes a more precise driving style possible.

On account of the greater share of the load borne by the back axle (the load distribution front to rear is 40 : 60) and the driving forces that have to be transmitted the rear tyres have to be considerably broader and bigger in order to accomplish all that is demanded of them, particularly the high temperatures.

There are only two tyre profiles : a completely smooth slick for all dry road surfaces and the strongly profiled rain tyre. In addition to their different looks, there are also differences in their rubber compound. In the middle of 1976 there were two slick compounds available : a relatively hard one with reduced grip but longer life – I credit my victory in the 1975 Swedish Grand Prix to this tyre – and a softer compound which really ought to be the universal racing tyre compound.

Dimensions

The size difference between front and rear tyres is best demonstrated by just looking at their vital statistics. Now that Goodyear enjoy a monopoly, they only manufacture front tyres sized 9,2/20.0 – 13 inches (or in millimetres : 234/508 – 330). For the rear axle too there is only one standard size : 16.2/26.0 – 13 inches (millimetres : 411/660 – 330). The first figure is always the tyre's width, the second its diameter and the third the rim diameter. From this we see that all four wheels have the same sized rims, 13 inches, but that their rolling circumference is considerably different because of the different tyre wall sizes. The rolling circumference of the front wheels is 1,595 millimetres, and of the rear wheels 2,074 millimetres. To take account of the differing tyre widths, the tyres are mounted on 10 inch (254 millimetre) wide rims in front and 17 inch (431 millimetre) wide rims in the rear.

On the rear wheels we sometimes experiment with 16 or 18 inch wide rims, which results in a somewhat paunchier or somewhat tauter tyre tension.

Compared with the tyre pressures we are accustomed to in road cars, the pressure in racing tyres is very low. We usually have 1.1 atmospheres (16 pounds per square inch) in front, 1.2 (18 pounds per square inch) in the rear. By altering this air pressure we can achieve only a very slight correction of the road handling (over- or under-steering). There is no way whatever of eradicating major road handling defects by simply varying the tyre pressures. In any case, the correct air pressure usually has to be determined on the basis of tyre temperature, as do the other wheel adjustment data like toe-in and camber. This temperature measurement is always made after a few fast practice laps by a tyre technician. A thermo-element on the tip of a needle probe is inserted at a shallow angle about 5 millimetres deep inside the rubber at three points on the tyre – centre, inside and outside edge. This probe is conveniently mounted in a handle, from which a cable leads to the actual display instrument which is calibrated in Centigrade or Fahrenheit. Of course we must not jab it in deep enough to damage the tyre's carcass let alone the airtight inner rubber layer. If the temperature varies across the cross-section we keep adjusting the camber, toe-in, anti-roll bar, air pressure and aerodynamic wing until the tyre temperature is approximately equal at all three points. Only this equal temperature distribution will enable us to exploit all a tyre's qualities – both its life and its grip – to the full.

The temperature will also tell us if the tyre (that is, its rubber compound) will be capable of standing the strain over the whole Grand Prix distance. If the temperature is above 110 degrees Centigrade we have to have resort to a harder compound, known as a 'back up compound'; this compound will always stand the strain but it will not give you such fast laps as the 'race compound'. It will be obvious that we use only 'race compound' during the practice laps that are so vital for our position on the starting grid; in earlier years there used to be super-soft 'qualifying tyres' that had to be thrown away after just three laps, but they do not make them any more now. Naturally when only one firm has a monopoly it does not want to know about such grotesque developments.

So although there are only two rubber compounds now, the decision which to use for a given race is tougher than it looks – for example Reutemann opted for the 'race compound' at the Swedish Grand Prix in 1975 and lost, while I took the 'back up compound' and won. I admit I had big problems keeping up with the other competitors in the early laps, but towards the end Reutemann began floundering around with his over strained tyres in such a way that I was able to make up for lost time and then overtake him too.

Basically the choice – soft or hard – depends on several factors. Will I have to drive the race flat out, will I be out ahead by myself or bunched up with the pack, will the actual race day be hotter or cooler than the practice laps, does the car or road surface change during the race? All this can have a big effect on a tyre's grip and useful life. The choice can be made even more complex by the fact that we can have two different compounds on the same car – in fact on the same axle, for that matter: as we drive clockwise round most tracks the left front tyre takes the biggest strain so we might select the harder compound just for that tyre, which will necessitate a lot of really precise adjustments.

Despite their monopoly Goodyear are working on further developments because nobody can say for certain that Firestone will not return or that Michelin or Pirelli will not start manufacture. Obviously Goodyear intend to keep their lead in case of that. In the course of tests that I myself frequently drive we are also confronted with new tyre designs and compounds. At the close of such tests these experimental tyres – that are usually very fast indeed – are immediately called in again so that no team will enjoy an unfair advantage over another at the next race meeting. If anybody did manage to sneak off with a set of these tyres he would still not be able to use them in a race because before the start of a race Goodyear technicians check all the tyre serials and the team's illicit enterprise would be punished by their not being supplied with any further Goodyear products, for example.

In these tyre tests we drive on tyres of different designs as well as compounds, for instance with greater or less sidewall rigidity and a consequent influence on the driving behaviour of the car. The big problem then is to re-adjust the car to suit these tyres so as still to get the best lap times. Different cars react in quite different ways to this. Basically we can say that we can exorcise a tendency to understeer by fitting front tyres of enhanced lateral rigidity. The car can then be steered more easily and exactly into bends.

We do get headaches, if for instance through faulty manufacture tyres of unequal size are fitted on one axle; this can happen even with brand new tyres. What happens then is even a car that has been perfectly set up and adjusted will take left-hand and right-hand curves differently – either under- or over-steering. To check for this fault we simply wrap a tape measure round the tyre, which enables us to measure its circumference most accurately. If the rear tyres are unequal in size, the car will always pull to one side on the straight; when we decelerate, the car then pulls to the other side.

Brand new tyres always have to be run in first, as it is like driving on ice with them at first. Only when the tyres have been roughened and warmed do they attain their maximum grip. They pass their optimum (super grip) period shortly after we begin using them : such a grip is available for only the first few laps and I always use it to try for the pole position. In this condition I can lap a circuit of 1 minute thirty seconds about half a second faster. After that the tyre wears down and approaches its normal grip, which it retains over its entire remaining useful life. The effect probably derives from some binding agent or other that is liberated when a new tyre is warmed up, making it briefly stickier than normal.

If the tyre is too strongly overheated during this super-grip phase it will blister : these rubber bubbles will then burst and make the tyre useless. Then the whole procedure of warming up has to be started all over again with new tyres. The whole thing is called 'heat treatment' too, and – without trying for pole position – it looks like this : fitting new tyres, warming them up for two or three laps, finally one lap flat out, back to the pits and letting the tyres cool off. Tyres treated like this are then usually ready for the whole Grand Prix distance.

In the actual race if the tyres are overstrained, mainly by persistent under-steering or full fuel tanks, we see an effect we know as 'graining' in racing jargon. Little granules of rubber build up on the tyres, just like on a rubber eraser, and these greatly diminish its grip. You can recognize this graining by a glance in the mirror at the back tyres or by looking at the front tyres : one segment of the tyre – usually the inner edge – is quite black. It would be absolutely wrong to keep on driving flat out because the effect gets worse and worse and spreads over the whole tyre tread. A few slower laps (one or two seconds slower) are then needed to rid the tyres of these granules so that they regain their full grip.

In cold weather there have been attempts to warm the tyres artificially before the start (Fittipaldi in Canada in 1974), in order to get the tyres up to the best working temperature from the word go. To prevent the tyres cooling down again during the last preparations for the start, they wrapped them in thick blankets. Despite all this effort I still won the starting duel with Fitti (we were both in the first row) although my own tyres had not been pre-warmed. Provided it is not really bitterly cold the warm-up lap before the start will be enough to bring the tyres up to the right temperature; besides which the Goodyear people are of the view that tyres warmed up on a moving car grip better than tyres that have been stuck in a sauna.

Rape of a tyre: either the load distribution from front to rear is wrong or sudden braking has caused the left front wheel of Vittorio Brambilla's March (in the centre) to lock. We can see that the wheel is not rotating as this is the only tyre on which we can clearly see slits marking the tread depth measurement. Because the wheel does not turn, the rubber in contact with the road surface has begun to heat up and melt, emitting clouds of smoke. The consequence will be powerful wheel vibrations.

The tyre size data are moulded into the wall of every racing tyre. This one is a rear tyre, with statistics in inches relating to the width, diameter and rim diameter. The picture also shows one of the eight safety bolts screwed like this into every rim (four internally, four externally) to stop the tyre shoulder jumping out of its seating on the wheel rim, if the tyre loses air pressure. Of course the bolt's thread has to be air tight in the rim, and the system can only be used with tubeless tyres. Readers may recall the TV pictures from the British 1974 Grand Prix at Brands Hatch, in which I was still able to drive on with one tyre completely in shreds, without losing control of the car. On this picture we can also see the tyre valve, which is simply screwed into the rim with two rubber washers. The black adhesive tape above the valve is to retain the balancing weight lying beneath it.

(Left). A new set of slicks is ready. Note the difference in size between front and wheel tyres. There are nine to twelve little slits cut into the tread of every slick to enable us to gauge how much tread is left in the centre and at the shoulders of the tyre (because of course there is no profile from which we can estimate this otherwise).

(Right). Rain tyres. If we look closely, we can see that the profile has in fact been hand cut.

A Goodyear technician measures the rolling circumference of a front tyre with a tape measure. Clearly visible here is the air box delivering cooling air to the brake disc concealed deep within the rim. The track rod passes through an opening provided in the box. This photograph was taken on a cold day (Daily Express trophy, Silverstone, 1975), so the air box opening has been two-thirds sealed off to prevent the brake discs getting too cold, when the surfaces would not attain the proper working temperature.

The tyre temperature is determined by inserting a needle probe (thermo element) into the tread rubber. The result is entered in a log and provides useful information on the wheel alignment.

GOOD**YEAR**

DATE	CAR	TIME

DRIVER _____

m.m.   m.m.

m.m.   m.m.

COMMENTS _____

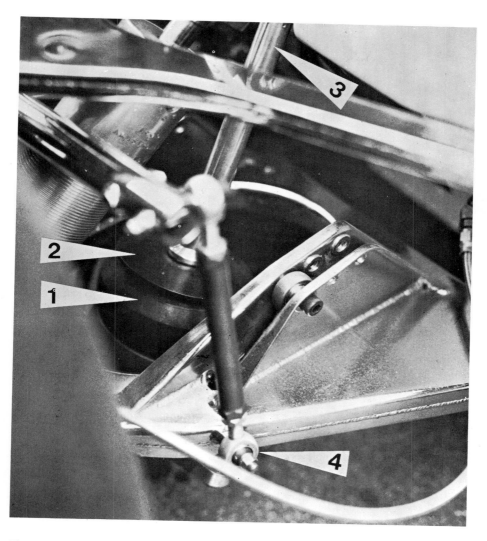

The interesting springing of the front wheel suspension of the Hesketh (1975 model). A rubber block (1) is set into the lower triangular wishbone, and is compressed when the springs are compressed. The rubber spring platform (2) is connected to the chassis by the linkage (3). While this rubber block does have its own damping properties, we are not able to dispense entirely with a shock absorber of the usual design (made here of aluminium, for weight reasons). Clearly visible in this picture: the lower ball joint (4) of the anti-roll bar linkage.

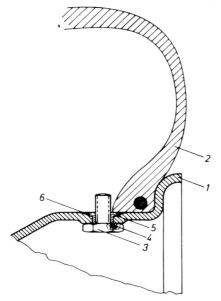

How the tyre safety bolt works. These bolts are distributed equidistantly round both the inner and outer sections of the rim. They prevent a tyre slipping off in the event of a defect. The bolts have to be unscrewed each time a tyre is put on or taken off. 1 : rim; 2 : tyre; 3 : safety bolt; 4 : airtight washer; 5 : threaded steel insert; 6 : metal adhesive.

Although the tyres on a Ferrari are mounted on three-section rims they can be put on and taken off without having to dismantle the rim. We only have to take out the safety bolts first. Unfortunately it does now and again happen that the tyres are not mounted squarely on the rims with the result that they get displaced during the drive. This would not be all that unpleasant were it not for the fact that the wheel's balance is then changed, causing the whole car to begin to vibrate. It is quite simple to check whether a tyre has become displaced like this: we just mark a line on the tyre and rim and check from time to time that the tyre has not slipped.

Vibrations may also be caused by one or more tyres on a car getting – paradoxically – not smaller but larger during a race. They pick up dirt and rubber granules that remain stuck to the tyre. Thanks to this 'pick up' as we call it I managed to end one race with a front tyre one centimetre bigger than when I started. As this pick up is not evenly distributed round the whole circumference, of course, the result will be vibrations that may be of such an intensity that you can barely grip the steering wheel any more because your wrists ache so much. Another consequence of the shaking up is that your visibility gets progressively worse – you are thrown about inside the cockpit so badly.

Another cause of vibrations is sudden braking that results in one wheel locking. The rubber is then subject to such intense local heat that it melts across an area the size of a tea plate, emitting the clouds of blue smoke familiar to all race watchers. We then detect the local flattening of the tyre by powerful vibrations immediately coming up the steering column. But that may be just the start of it: if the heat developed is too intense the rubber may develop bubbles where it has been flattened, and begin to peel: it 'blisters'. If the race has much longer to run then there can be no thought of driving to the finish like that – there is nothing for it but to go to the pits for a tyre change.

86

Rain Tyres

In contrast to dry weather tyres, rain tyres have a very pronounced profile. Because rain tyres are only seldom needed, this profile is cut by hand in tyres that are originally smooth : it would be uneconomical to purchase a machine to do this. Besides, you are always learning new things about how to cut this profile. The second difference with respect to dry weather tyres is in their rubber compound : the wet tyre compound is considerably softer.

There are worlds of difference between driving a car with dry and rain tyres. We could never even dream of lapping a dry track with rain tyres as fast as we do with slicks. And we lose even more time driving on a wet track with

The car presented by Hesketh in 1975 took the spring story one step further: the entire front wheel suspension was worked out on the basis of rubber springing. As the front wheels are largely masked by the aerodynamic nose, the regular ventilation boxes for the front brake discs proved ineffective; so here the air is inducted through two airboxes lying close to the car body and fed through hoses to the brakes.

The 1975 Hesketh also boasted an interesting rubber system for the rear springs instead of the usual coil spring system. We can clearly recognize the engine's actual load bearing function in this picture, from the way that one side of the spring-system's support is fastened directly to the cylinder head (1). On the other side there is an improved welded device (2) that simultaneously contains the bearing for the stabilizer (the version here is a bent tube) and provides a support for the inner ball joint (3) of the upper wishbone.

slicks – particularly if there are already puddles – and in borderline situations we can only drive at a walking pace because of the risk of aquaplaning. If the track is already drying out we will usually be faster with the slicks than with rain tyres, so there is no profit to be made from waiting until it is bone dry before heading for the pits for a tyre change.

If the pits are not ready for a tyre change for some reason or other and I am forced to carry on for one or more laps on rain tyres although the track is

The Ferrari 312 T's front suspension. The internal springing arrangement was primarily opted for so as to leave free access for the air stream to the two radiators. The main parts of the wheel suspension are mounted on a strong plate of magnesium (1). The rack-and-pinion steering, brake cylinders and two brake-fluid reservoirs are also mounted on this plate. The upper wishbones (2) have to be stiffened against bending moments in this case, as they not only have to locate the wheel but also have to act on the internal springs. Obviously this makes the wishbones that much heavier, but this disadvantage is offset by one particular refinement: normally the anti-roll bar would have to cross the entire chassis width to pick up the spring movements on the wheel suspensions; but this is dealt with much more elegantly – and more importantly at far less weight – here: the spring movements are transferred to the centre of the car in any case, so only the shortest of torsion bars (3) is called for to act as an anti-roll bar. By means of two linkages (like the one visible at 4) two levers are operated which work the spline of the torsion bar. These levers have several notches to allow us to enhance or reduce the effect of the anti-roll bar; and of course we can also insert torsion bars of different strengths.

Rear Wheel Suspension
The Ferrari 312 T's rear wheel suspension, consisting of a radius rod (1), a lower wishbone (2), an upper link (3, half obscured by the pipeline), the magnesium upright (4) and the anti-roll bar (5).

> *The form usually taken by the rear anti-roll bar in Formula cars, in this case the Ferrari 132 T. The torsion bar (1) is acted on by two levers. To prevent the levers simply twisting round the bar they are splined at the joint and rigidly locked together. Each lever has five holes (2), into which the ball joint of the linkage can be inserted to provide for different anti-roll bar effects. As shown here, the anti-roll bar has been adjusted to its softest point (the last hole provides the maximum effect leverage). Notice particularly on this picture the bright patches round the edge of the left internally-cooled brake disc: these are patches of various paint colours that have the property of changing colour at different high temperatures. In this way the operating temperature of the brake disc can be determined and if need be the ventilation shaft leading to the brake disc can be opened up or closed to adjust it.*

already dry, then I quite deliberately drive outside the normal driving line, at least on the straights, so as not to overheat the very soft rubber compound of the rain tyres. Outside the 'off line' the surface is still relatively wet so the tyres will be better cooled. It is only a little trick, but it helps me get over the dangerous transition period without losing too much time.

Wet tyres are only manufactured to the same sizes as slicks. There are no such things as all weather tyres ('intermediates') because if the weather is uncertain Grand Prix races are not started anyway – the race is delayed until either it is definitely raining or (preferably) definitely dry.

SUSPENSION

After the tyres the suspension is the next link between the car and the road surface. The suspensions of the various Formula I cars are remarkably similar and the roll centres of the front and back axles barely differ from one car to the next. On account of the broad tyres and various design features adopted in recent years the following basic principles have been adopted: independent wheel suspensions front and rear with an upper and lower triangular wishbone on the front axle and one or two radius rods used in conjunction with wishbones on the rear.

There are no genuine design differences, just variations on the theme: for instance the front axle wishbones may be tubular or square sections; in the rear they may be simple triangular wishbones or the trapezium sort. In every case our endeavour is to design the wheel suspension so that each component is subject only to compressive and tensile forces (i.e., not to bending moments) which makes the design much simpler to calculate. Obviously we design as economically as possible, both to cut down on the car's overall weight and to keep the unsprung mass as low as possible. Even so steel is the material most used; only half-hearted experiments have been made with other metals like aluminium, magnesium or titanium.

Although the Ferrari does have a weight problem, there is something approaching an aversion to dabbling with new metals. This is probably attributable to a guiding principle of Enzo Ferrari: he once said, 'There is no such

Incomparable Barcelona: Entry into the Arena of Montjuich.
Clay Regazzoni.
Barcelona, 1975.
Pits: Regazzoni, Myself/Jarier.

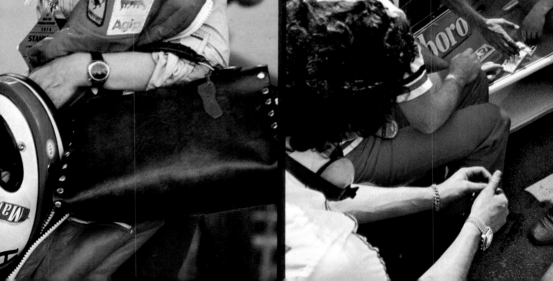

thing as a Ferrari that loses a wheel'. My own personal view is that there need not necessarily be a connection between these two facts provided the thing is approached in the right way. We only have to look at the success that other much heavier cars have had with light non-ferrous metals – BMW and Ford touring cars, the Porsche GT – and they do not go around shedding wheels.

At any rate I do what I can to direct our technicians' attention to new materials, so as to get rid of our weight handicap as soon as we can.

There is much more variety as far as springs are concerned, both in the design and in its material execution. As a rule progressive coil springs are used, usually encasing the shock absorbers. Ferrari and some other firms use titanium for the manufacture of the body springs, because it is a light metal and its different qualities from those of steel make it particularly suitable.[1]

Other firms used torsion bars front and rear (Lotus), while Hesketh has recently gone over to using rubber blocks. This means doing away with coil springs completely, though not of course with shock absorbers; but it gives them large possibilities of selecting the right springing by employing different grades of rubber and different shapes.

We find similar rubber blocks, though of smaller dimensions, in the conventional springing too : here they serve as platforms for the spring elements. Proper dimensioning here is vital, as the rubber has to bear some of the load and support the coil springs when the car is well down, e.g., with full petrol tanks.

As far as the torsion bar suspension used in some cars is concerned, it is very costly, but its advantage lies in having the lowest possible centre of gravity.

Back to the conventional spring elements. On the back axle they are mounted facing diagonally outwards : that is, they are fastened at the top to the chassis and at the outside bottom to the wheel suspension or wishbones. On the front axle some teams use inboard suspension, other teams outboard suspension. The advantage of inboard elements is diminished wind resistance because the space between chassis and front wheels remains uncluttered for the air stream passing between them; the disadvantage however is the increased construction cost,

[1] Titanium's elasticity coefficient is only half that of steel, which means that a titanium component will distort twice as much as a steel component of identical dimensions and loading. Titanium is therefore twice as elastic as steel which makes it particularly suitable for vehicle springs, as we need only half the number of coil windings. A further advantage : titanium is 40 per cent lighter than steel. Titanium is not suitable for components that have to be particularly rigid (like the crankshaft); besides titanium has poor gliding qualities, it wears out every roller bearing. Finally : titanium is much dearer than steel and more difficult to work with. There are high-grade titanium alloys but they are even less rigid than high-grade steel alloys. So even titanium is no miracle metal.

because the wheel's up and down movements now have to be transmitted to the spring elements inside the chassis. Ferrari have developed a very special solution to this problem (see the photo on page 89).

The shock absorbers work on the same principle as on normal road cars, but are of much more costly manufacture so as to enable us to adjust their damping characteristics in both compression and tension rapidly. Single-tube gas-pressure shock absorbers are not used despite their numerous advantages because we cannot adjust them from outside. To obtain a different degree of damping we would have to change the entire spring assembly each time, which would take a lot of time and considerably increase the spare-part requirement.

Given a properly designed vehicle it is in fact a matter of course that it will attain a neutral road handling once it has been suitably adjusted. But this in turn requires that all the main suspension elements of each wheel can be independently adjusted, in other words :
O adjustment of the aluminium spring-platforms on the coils of the shock absorbers so that the car body clears the ground front and rear;
O adjustment of spring tension by changing the springs;
O adjustment of shock absorbers' compression and tension either by turning a wheel on the shock absorbers or by bodily exchanging them;
O toe in on the front axle by twisting the two track rods;
O castor angle of the front wheels by longitudinally displacing the upper or lower outer wishbone points;
O camber of the front wheels by transverse displacement of the upper or lower wishbone points.
O toe-in on the back axle by adjusting the wishbone points;
O camber of the back wheels by adjusting the upper or lower wishbone points transversely;
O changes of load distribution when the car rolls, by changing the anti-roll bar setting or fitting different anti-roll bars front and rear.

The car will have all these basic adjustments made after its assembly while still in the factory. This operation is performed on a big level platform. (But these adjustments may be affected later on by the vehicle springs settling, the bearings in the joints wearing loose, or if the car hits kerbstones, guard rails and the like.) For this dead accurate works adjustment the car is fitted not with the usual thick rubber tyres but with narrow aluminium discs of precisely the same diameter as the tyres; these discs are then bolted on instead of the wheel rims. This makes the adjustments easier and excludes all possibility of error due to tyre or air pressure differences.

After this basic setting-up of the car, it is placed – still on the aluminium discs – on four scales to measure the wheel loadings. If everything is all right, the two scales on each axle must each show the same load. Minor adjustments can be made by screwing the spring platforms up or down. If this weighing procedure has to be performed in the pits at a race track, for example after a minor accident, it is often difficult to find a level enough surface. So we then put up four little platforms and carefully level them, and the car is then rolled on to them.

In test drives we examine the influence of other factors – like adjustments to the roll centres – on the car's behaviour, in addition to the adjustments to the factors we have already mentioned which do have a considerable effect on it. Contrary to what one might expect, such changes affect the car's behaviour only a very little. Over the years the optimum geometrical conditions have been arrived at almost by themselves with the result that nowadays virtually every Formula I car has the same kind of suspension.

The wings provide a further way of varying the car's road behaviour.

Diagnosing Faults

The individual effects will be these :
- Too little toe-in on the front axle : the car brakes unevenly.
- Too much toe-in : excessive heating of the tyres' inner edges.
- Too little toe-in on the rear axle : car's road handling unsteady.
- Springs too soft : car rolls too strongly on bends.
- Springs too hard : car does not roll enough, diminished reaction to anti-roll bars, car skips excessively over surface ridges.
- Shock absorbers too soft : car dips abruptly on entering bend and hits the rubber stops on the wheel suspension, understeers into corners.
- Shock absorbers too hard : car skips over surface ridges and reacts poorly to the two anti-roll bars when the car's direction is rapidly changed.
- Too much castor : car difficult to steer.
- Too little castor : little steering effort necessary but road contact poor.
- Too much camber in front : oversteers.
- Too little camber in front : understeers.
- Too much camber in rear : understeers.
- Too little camber in rear : oversteers.
- Front anti-roll bar too soft : oversteers.
- Front anti-roll bar too hard : understeers.

99

○ Rear anti-roll bar too soft : understeers.
○ Rear anti-roll bar too hard : oversteers.

And now to the wings which – particularly on bends – determine how a car will handle. The following rule applies : the more wing (i.e., the sharper the wing angle) the lower the top speed but the greater the down-pressure and hence the greater the acceptable centrifugal force; but also the greater the rolling resistance of the tyres.

Too much wing in front will result in oversteering; too much wing in the rear results in understeering.

We hardly ever alter the car's ground clearance and then only by very little (10 millimetres for the Nürburgring). If there is any risk of grounding we prefer to put an extra underbody protection. Otherwise we can also raise the rubber bump stops on the car's springs.

Every Formula car has an anti-roll bar front and rear and changing these has a powerful effect on the car's handling. Basically speaking we can get the same effect by making the rear anti-roll bar harder than we can by making the front softer, and vice versà. So in certain circumstances we quite deliberately turn our attention only to one of the two anti-roll bars. For instance if the car strongly oversteers when we accelerate out of a bend, we will make the rear anti-roll bar softer. This has the effect of giving the inner wheel more ground pressure, enabling the back axle to accept more lateral pressures and counteract the tendency to oversteer. Only when we cannot adjust that anti-roll bar any more do we turn to the other method, of making the front anti-roll bar harder – thereby diminishing the front axle's ability to accept lateral pressures and achieving the same end effect.

As the anti-roll bars are softened, the car's roll when taking corners will increase. I personally prefer driving a car that rolls to a certain extent (as it provides for better road holding) but it must not be taken too far. Particularly at chicanes – when the track rapidly zigzags to left and right – the car will then roll too fast until the rubber bump stops check the roll. This results in a distinctly bumpy and irritable ride which is certainly not what is wanted.

At the other extreme are anti-roll bars that have been made too hard. While they do limit the tendency to roll and simplify driving, in my view they do not permit the fastest laps because when the car does roll to one side the springing is thereby over-compressed resulting in an early loss of road contact if there are surface ridges. Of course, a car's handling is also a factor of the hardness of the car's main springs – coil springs in the case of the Ferrari – but when the proper hardness of these has once been found these are scarcely ever altered afterwards.

A remarkable photograph from the 1975 season showing three cars, each handling completely differently. My Ferrari (Number 12) is absolutely neutral; Jody Scheckter's Tyrrell (Number 3) is slightly oversteering, and Fittipaldi's Mclaren (Number 1) is heavily understeering.

From all this it is clear that the proper adjustment of a car is a highly technical job for the driver. It must also be made plain that in actual practice the various effects are by no means as obvious as we have described. Any one adjustment may produce a series of undesirable side-effects in addition to the desired effect, which only complicates things more. Inevitably the point comes when all the driver's personal sensitivity is of no further avail : he has to allow the stop-watch to decide the pros and cons of any given alteration. This is why it is absolutely vital that after every such alteration three or four high speed laps must be driven. The stop-watch times that result provide objective evidence one way or the other.

Driving

There is something of a ceremony about starting and warming up a Formula I engine – but naturally even this is all dictated by sound technical considerations. Usually the mechanics take care of all that and I am able to sit down in a car that is all ready to go. But sometimes when we are short of time and I am already sitting in the car for some reason or other, I take charge of the pre-liminaries myself.

STARTING AND WARMING UP

To spare the car's own battery an outside battery is plugged in to the car's rapid connecting socket to provide the juice for starting. Then a mechanic operates the main switch to the right of the wing support, behind the car's battery. After the ignition has been turned on by the appropriate switch on the steering wheel, the oil pressure warning light must light up just as on any other car. A glance at the fuel pressure indicator will show whether the switch operated electric petrol pump is delivering enough pressure for the injection system. When the starter button is pressed the engine ought to fire without any nonsense, whereupon the oil pressure light will at once go out and the oil pressure indicator will rise to about 9 kp per square centimetre. I might add that the fuel/air mixture is enriched for the entire start procedure by means of a simple manual adjustment to the injection pump.

After the engine first starts we only give just enough gas to avoid letting the oil pressure exceed 10 kp per square centimetre, otherwise the cold (and hence viscous) oil might cause damage to the various oil pipes or the oil filter. At this time the revs will be around 3,000 rpm – in other words still below the rev counter's range.

Once the oil and water have reached about 60 degrees Centigrade we slowly push up the revs and begin doing what we Austrians call *melken* – blipping the throttle, to open and close the throttle-slide in rapid succession either using the accelerator pedal or applying one finger direct to the engine. The reason for this blipping the throttle is to prevent the spark plugs oiling up as they otherwise might when the engine is running at constant revs on an enriched mixture. (I have already mentioned that we do not use the so-called warm-up plugs any more as the swap-over in a Ferrari would take so much time and labour that it just would not be worth the effort.)

If the outside temperature is very low the two oil coolers and two radiators are first sealed off with sticky tape to prevent the slipstream from cooling down the engine too much. In Formula I cars we do not have a thermostat like those in production models to keep the temperature constant, it would only be a further possible cause of defects and a further complication of the technical interplays. The first laps on a practice day are in any case only used for instrument checks and never for any great acts of courage : so we keep a close watch on the oil and water temperatures and return to the pits if they are not right – we can regulate them in any direction we want by putting on or taking off strips of sticky tape on the radiators.

On these first laps we particularly heed any kind of noises, especially if it is a new engine that we have just installed. From experience we very soon recognize in this way if the engine is running smoothly or if, for instance it is missing on one cylinder or there are 'impermissible' engine vibrations. What is quite obvious is that in such a case you do not carry on and hope for the best, but send in the mechanics; equally, you will be doing them a favour if you can describe the fault as precisely as possibly – and perhaps even offer a diagnosis.

The slow warm-up, of two or three laps of average length, does the motor and all other moving parts good because cold oils (gear box) and grease (wheel bearings) are poor lubricants.

When the car is well warmed up and the temperatures are right (around 85 degrees for water and 80 degrees for oil) we check whether the engine runs smoothly right through the rpm range and whether the rev limiter operates at the pre-set limit. We can make adjustments in the first case to the injection pump, and in the second by means of a small adjusting screw.

After that we have reached the point when we can set off for a few fast laps.

The PVC air trumpet conducts cooling air into the centre of the wheel
bearing and thence into the brake disc. The cooling channels in the brake disc
are of spiral shape. On this photograph we can also see the wheel hub – in
racing one central nut is the most usual fastening. The four studs visible next
to the threaded hub slip into holes on the wheel to prevent it rotating against
the brake disc.

Braking

In Formula I design a lot of work has been done on the brake systems – as was both right and proper, I might add. In any case they hardly ever cause trouble and they are very reliable – provided we pay them due attention during the running in period.

All Formula I cars have internally air cooled disc brakes on all four wheels. The rear discs are inside the car body, in fact they are right next to the differential and the brake callipers are bolted directly on to it. Today on all cars the front discs are external, either next to or in the wheel rim. Until lately Lotus had its front brake discs inside the body. All the brakes are provided with a stream of cooling air deflected by air boxes : the air is directed at the centre of the disc, which is open on the inside face, and from there the air streams through the cooling channels provided in the disc. Obviously such cooling systems have been provided more for the really hot days, and they are sealed up when the outside temperature drops very low as the discs must not get too cold either. To determine whether they are reaching their proper temperature, several special patches are painted on their outer edge during practice laps; these change colour quite definitely in accordance with the temperatures reached, so we can be certain whether the cooling is right or not.

The brake pads are extremely heat resistant and still retain a lot of their braking power even way above 500 degrees Centigrade. But these too – like the tyres – need a special warming-up treatment first. As new pads make an enormous difference and call for a completely different driving technique we drivers are expressly warned when our mechanics have put in a new set. In my own case I am warned by a red sticky tape on my steering wheel. Running in new brake pads has to be done with extreme caution. First we warm up the pads quite slowly, by extending all braking-distances to two or three times their normal length. So if my normal braking point is 50 yards before a particular curve, with the new pads I put my foot down 150 yards before the curve and quite gently at that. On an average track I will carry on like this usually for four laps. During this period the car will be braking exceptionally poorly and the pads will be emitting a foul stink (which is perceptible not only behind the car but in the cockpit too, quite clearly). The brake pedal reacts quite stiffly (the same point of brake contact, but poor retarding). After this initiation period the brake pads then have to be given a kind of shock treatment – they have to be overheated. I do this by stamping on the brakes at top speed, causing the pedal to go soggy (fading). After that I drive one or two laps quite slowly again to allow the pads to cool down – and then they are ready for the race. You can only seriously consider setting out on a Grand Prix race with pads treated like this : in the course of the actual race virtually the entire pad thickness (10 millimetres) will be worn out.

If we have not warmed up the pads enough during the running in, they will glaze over and be useless until this glaze has been rubbed off. If they get too hot, bits of pad will simply flake right off. When they are functioning just right – and that is usually the case – the brakes will keep their performance so that no fading is perceptible at any phase of the race, not even in the very last laps.

In the Ferrari the brake systems are practically the same size front and rear (the same brake callipers, pistons and discs), which is evidence enough of the importance attached to the rear brakes.

For optimum braking it is obviously important to distribute brake pressure correctly between front and rear. The adjustment is made on the two master cylinders (one for rear, one for front) which lie next to each other. The two brake pistons are operated by one balance-beam, with the pedal force being applied at a point approximately at the centre of this beam. By adjusting this point to left or right we can send more brake pressure to one axle and less to the other. In a single seater car, of course, you can clearly see your own back wheels too in the rear mirror, so you can see just how much each wheel is retarded by the brakes and thereby make corrections to the brake-pressure distribution.

In the event that one brake circuit collapses, there is a stop on this balance-beam so that all available brake pressure then goes over to the cylinder of the still-intact brake circuit.

As for wet tracks, what we must do is quite obvious : give more brake pressure to the back axle.

DRIVING ON THE STRAIGHT

It sounds daft, but the question is not as silly as it sounds : are there any difficulties in driving a Formula I car on the straight? In theory there should not be, but in practice there sometimes are – firstly when there is something wrong with the wheel geometry and secondly when the tyres are cold. Cold tyres play up on the slightest surface irregularity; instead of driving straight they zigzag – and any attempt at driving fast means taking your life in your own

On the straight: on a smooth surface (here it is at Kyalami) driving is no problem . . .

hands. Tyres only get full elasticity when they reach proper driving temperature, and only this enables us to drive precisely and without risk.

On cold days – and in racing this means barely above freezing point – the tyres will never reach their best working temperature: then it is impossible to take the uneven-surfaced straight at Brands Hatch flat out because the car would just spin out of control; and of course it is equally impossible to drive precisely into the bends in such circumstances.

When the tyres are in normal condition driving on the straight on tracks like Zeltweg with its particularly level surface is child's play. Anybody can do it. At the other extreme there is the Interlagos track in Brazil, where we have to pay as much attention on the straights as on the curves. What is particularly bad is when there is a difference in level between the various asphalt lanes: even if it is only a very tiny difference, running parallel to your direction of travel, you are best advised to try and position this ridge exactly between your wheels

. . . but it certainly is on the switchback at Interlagos.

because when you actually touch the ridge your car slips sideways in a distinctly nasty manner.

A further problem that may arise on the straight is wind buffeting, particularly clearings in forests that suddenly let the wind hit the track (for example at Monza just before the Curva Grande). In a strong wind you may suddenly find your car thrown two or even three yards off course; the worst thing is the first time it hits you, when you have got to get over your own surprise as well.

GEAR CHANGE

The straightforward act of changing gear presents no problem, especially where the Ferrari is concerned. But this means that the gear linkage must be exactly adjusted and it must work properly – and this is by no means a matter of course in Formula I cars where the gearbox is right at the back and the driver is sitting as far forward as possible, because the gear linkage between them has got several hurdles to clear (the engine, for instance!) This means using little universal joints that have as little free play as possible, enabling us to alter the angle of the gear linkage properly. As described earlier, on the Ferrari there is a metal gate to guide the gear lever, so we can always see which particular gear has been selected at any moment.

It is difficult to change gear until the gearbox has reached its proper working temperature, because the cold gear oil is very viscous still. Apart from this the gear change requires little effort – and of course it must be done as fast as possible. In view of the enormous acceleration power of a Formula I car every tenth of a second lost changing gear is obviously of vital importance. We can cut this loss of time by shortening the travel of the clutch pedal and the gear lever. The clutch is adjusted so that even when the pedal is depressed only a few millimetres it is declutched, and the gear lever travel from one gear to the next is also exceptionally short – only about ten millimetres, measured at the gear lever knob.

Because speed means everything we dispense with synchromesh, so we have to double declutch when changing down – you do it absolutely automatically after you get used to it.

We only select first gear just before driving off; in other words we start up in neutral and keep in it until the last checks (air pressure, securing the body flaps) have been carried out and we get the Okay sign from the man who is in charge. Putting it in gear causes a scraping sound and the car shudders slightly, so you can actually feel that power is being transmitted now to the gearbox.

There is no way of cutting out the noise, but it is of no further importance. The noise is less irritating the lower the revs when first gear is selected, but if we take the revs too low we run the risk of the engine dying on us.

If I am slogging away or driving fast practice laps, I will always leave changing up to the very last moment – i.e., when the revs reach the maximum of 12,300 rpm. As we will have picked the gear ratios during practice laps to fit the vagaries of each track exactly, I will have the satisfaction of knowing that when I change down to take each bend the rev jump will be just right when I let in the clutch again. So, provided I have not selected the wrong gear by mistake, it will not be possible for the engine to over-rev when I change back.

AIRBORNE

One of the very few opportunities of seeing today's Formula I cars airborne: between the Pflanzgarten and the Swallowtail on the Nürburgring (this photo shows the late Carlos Pace's Brabham in 1974). The wheel springs are fully extended. The driver has to take his foot off the accelerator immediately to avoid over-revving his engine. Note that these tyres are paunchier than usual because of their very high velocity of rotation, as the car is doing about 160 mph.

If I find I have got a big enough lead in a race, then I mentally set myself a lower rev limit to change gear at, one lying about 200 or 300 rpm lower.

Taking to the Air

Cars do not go airborne so much as they used to in Grand Prix races. Modern Formula I cars are just not designed for spectacular aerobatics. Their aerodynamic wings have increased the down pressure on the cars to such an extent that you will only see them really leaving the ground nowadays at two tracks – at the Nürburgring (in two places) and in Barcelona. For these tracks some cars have their underbodies reinforced with magnesium plating to prevent them being damaged on 'touchdown'.

The most important rule to remember when the car takes off is this : decelerate, because if the rear wheels race it may over-rev the engine. The second point to remember is to try to take off squarely and to land squarely, as otherwise you will start zigzagging on touchdown and you will lose time sorting yourself out again.

As the cars have not exactly been designed with these aerobatics in mind, it may well be that a car has poor flying qualities and acts up nastily when it lands. Today this is of less importance, as your flying time is only a tiny fraction of the total lap. In other words we do not start tinkering around with the car's toe-in or shock absorbers to suit the car for its brief airborne existence, provided the car is otherwise okay.

CORNERING

For me taking a corner begins at that instant in time when the acceleration is abruptly interrupted – when my right foot changes as fast as possible from accelerator to brake pedal. You work out empirically the exact spot to begin braking during practice laps, and then you mentally record certain landmarks so you can find the spot next time. In practice there's a landmark for each such curve, either a notice or something unusual about a guard rail or the safety fence. As you can also think in terms of 'just before' this landmark, or 'just after' that, you can always memorize the position of each curve's braking point.

It is the same as driving a normal car : you cannot just stamp on the brakes like a madman, otherwise the wheels will block. I push the pedal down relatively lightly until I feel the pressure point, and then – and only then – I put my weight into it. In this way I have the entire braking procedure tightly under control.

You normally stop braking when you steer into the curve. At the same moment you begin accelerating again to keep the car's radial velocity constant or to accelerate it out of the curve again.

If the car is understeering my own practice is to keep braking into the curve, as this will offset the car's tendency to keep going straight ahead. But this 'braking into the curve' is admittedly a ticklish business because it leaves you practically no room for correction if you have bitten off more than you can chew. (Driving an oversteering car like this is not possible – it would spin round immediately.)

Steering into the curve is done either gently or more violently, according to the type of car. There are the more sullen cars that need to be thrown in by brute force. My old model, the B3, was one-such car. Steering the Ferrari 312 T is much simpler, the car is much better at cornering.

Actually braking while in the curve – the sin against which every ordinary motorist is rightly warned – does occasionally occur in racing driving. Mainly it is when you have begun accelerating out of the curve prematurely, causing the nose to ride up and the front wing to deliver less down pressure in consequence (because its angle of adjustment is no longer correct). You then have to tap the brakes briefly to tilt the car forwards again, which corrects the down-pressure again and the car will not understeer any longer.

In drawing a distinction between cars that corner well and badly, I must add that there are also differences caused by the curves themselves : in relation to understeering and oversteering. This was already referred to in the technical introduction to this book – the fact that a car's handling can be influenced almost *ad infinitum* by the various adjustments possible, to camber, stabiliser, wings : of course our endeavour is to make the car as neutral in its handling as possible. When you are accelerating powerfully out of a bend, however, using a lot of engine power, you can never entirely avoid a certain amount of oversteering. The more this can be prevented, the sooner you will get the full power of your engine back onto the track again.

There have been whole books full of diagrams and discussions about the 'ideal line' in which to take a particular curve. My own view is that all such theories are very good for the theoreticians, but in practice they are quite valueless.

If you just look at any particular curve on a Grand Prix track, you will see that every driver follows precisely the same line, and you will realize that there is no other sensible possibility anyway. Any racing driver who is even half

The Ideal Line in practice: not an art, it just happens.

worth his salt will find this ideal line automatically – if the car is driven fast enough it will 'tell him' it wants to follow that line, but even if it did not, there is no room for any individualism: apart from on the very first days of a brand new racing track, the ideal line is not just some theoretical line but a very concrete factor indeed: because it will be the only clean driving surface left round any particular curve – the cars sweep all the rubber granules and other foreign bodies like pebbles and sand off this ideal line as they hurtle round it, and this debris lies to either side of it. You could only venture on to the debris zones at drastically reduced speeds, because if you are forced off the ideal line for any reason your tyres immediately lose grip and you have some very nasty moments keeping the car on course. Under such conditions there could be no thought of driving really fast round the corner. You will find out soon enough just how much this debris affects you if you have to leave the ideal line to lap a slower driver (if need be you will *lap* him on a bend if you can rely on him to give way; but you can only *overtake* on the straights or in braking zones, and

The Ideal Line itself is easily visible from the track marked by the (more heavily loaded) outer wheels.

then you will often have a parallel lane to drive in so the difference is not so great). If you leave the right track when you are lapping somebody, the result will be that your hot and sticky tyres will pick up the dirt and you will notice the effect on the car at once – you just have to drive slower. Your tyres will only be clean again after an average of two more laps on the clean road surface, allowing you to resume your original speed. If you are using a soft rubber compound however you may well find that you just cannot get rid of the dirt at all – on the contrary, the tyres pick up more and more and grow bigger and bigger. As we mentioned in the chapter on tyres this may result in vibrations that will grow worse and worse as time goes on.

To return once more to this notion of an 'ideal line' : the time is past when you could slice tenths of seconds off your time by particularly clever selection of an ideal line, let alone win a race that way. So in my view there is no point in theorizing on it. You may be disappointed not to find any of those famous diagrams in this book, showing dotted lines, 'apexes' and so on; but believe me, it is a waste of time. The fastest driver today is the man who can angle and adjust his car just right so that it drives fastest along the only possible line there is – the line that you find out yourself soon enough after very little practice.

Very many bends on race tracks are edged with 'curbs', which rise steeply towards the outer edge and form the narrow outer lane of a curve. They are just right for catching an oversteering car accelerating out of a curve, because you can let your outer wheel drift on to this elevated portion. In this case it is important not to take your foot off the accelerator, so as to keep the car stable. Regazzoni once made the mistake of doing just that on a 'curb' in trial drives at Paul Ricard – he ended up with the wreckage of his car in the safety fence. Any driving on the 'curbs' on straights, on the entry into a bend or at its inner apex is absolutely wrong as it will abruptly throw the car off course, which means you will go off your ideal line.

There is also a very unpleasant kind of 'curb' that you have to avoid even when drifting outwards – those where a distinct ridge occurs where the track surface meets the curb. For instance on the Nürburgring track the curb ends with a vertical two-inch drop to the track surface, so the wheel would have to clear first of all a two-inch high ridge with highly unfavourable effects on the

On this picture the 'curbs' bordering the actual track surface are clearly visible. Normally you would only drive over one in a real slogging match – as Emerson Fittipaldi is doing here – because you are risking damage to the suspension.

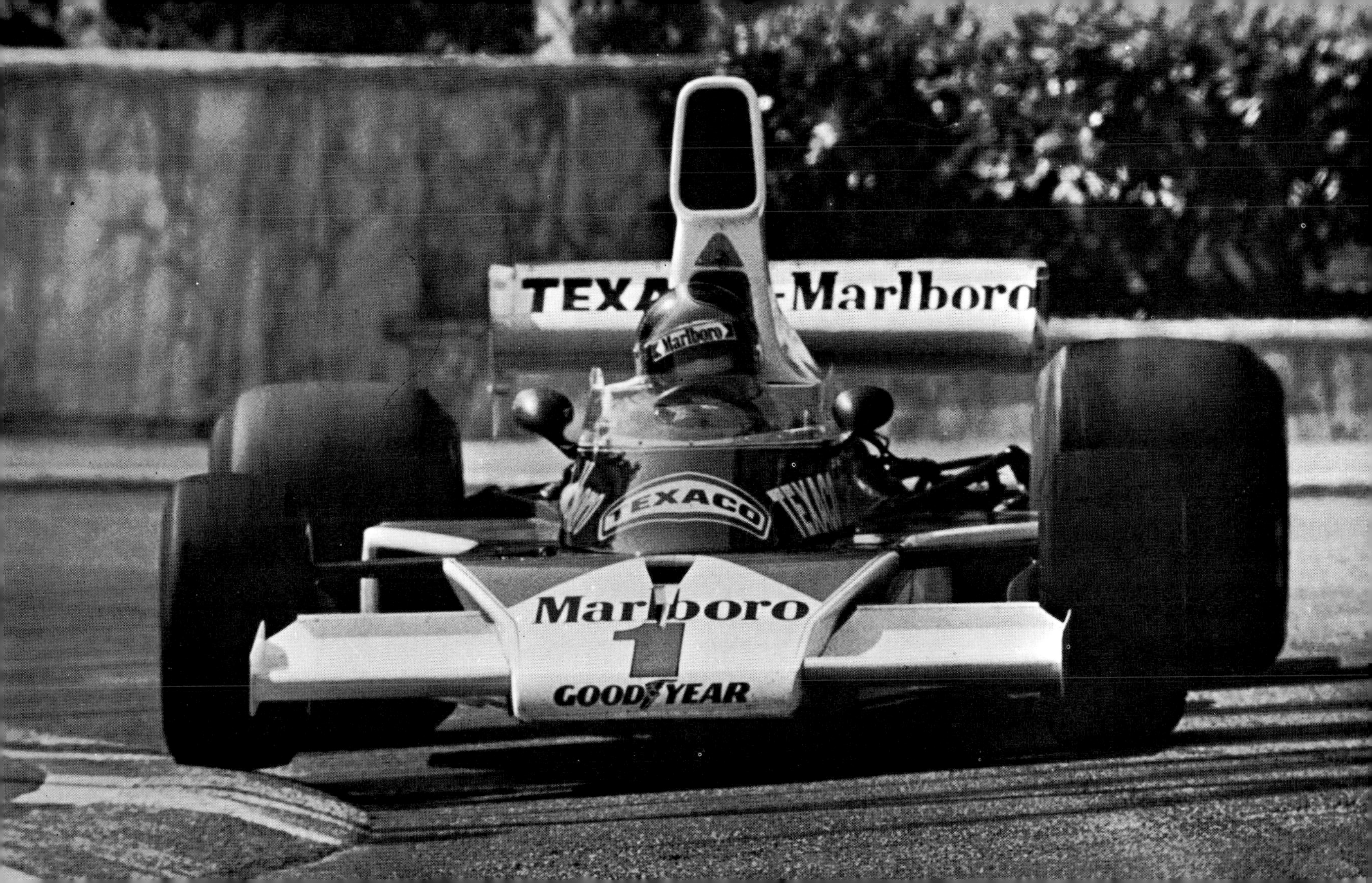
Marlboro
TEXACO
Marlboro
1
GOODYEAR

suspension, let alone on the car's handling – the car would react very unsteadily to crossing the ridge.

Is there any way of getting out of crisis situations on bends? There are two basic possibilities. If you steer into a bend and the car begins oversteering so badly that you know you will go into a spin any moment, one thing you can do is suddenly give short sharp bursts of power; of course if you have begun spinning already nothing will help you. These short power bursts will give the rear wheels more grip again and this may just enable you to regain control of the car.

If a spin is inevitable, in most cases you will stamp on the brakes so as to be able to decide at least the direction that your car will be flung out. Because if you do this, your car will then shoot tangentially out of the curve and end up somewhere out of the firing line of the car right behind you – and somewhere where, we will hope, there are big enough crash spaces waiting for you. You will usually find afterwards that there is no trace on the tyres of the wheels having locked when you braked, because your spin will have begun outside the ideal line – i.e. in the dirty lanes where your tyres were not gripping anyway.

The time available for the decision – do I tread on the accelerator or on the brakes? – is incredibly short : in fact you will always act instinctively one way or the other. Obviously, to try and get out of the emergency by short sharp bursts of power is a risky way, because if it does not come off you are going to wind up with a much higher terminal velocity than if you relied on the spin-and-brake method.

COMBINATION CURVES

We often hear people talk about combination curves. Usually they are talking about a sequence of bends in which when taking one you do not have to worry about the next one. Real combinations of such curves only occur in fact at the Nürburgring, in Monaco (the station and Portier) and at Mosport in Canada.

With such combinations I try to decide during my study of the track (either in my own private car, or a race car or on a map) which bend in the combination is the most important. Usually it is the last one, because I will want to accelerate into the following straight as fast as possible.

If it is a genuine combination curve you will not really notice it unless you get into difficulties in it. You will suddenly find yourself cornering too fast and

Proper respect for the 'curbs' at Monaco: Jochen Mass.

you have lost the ideal line: then you can only make for the emergency exit. It is like a slalom in which you are travelling just too fast to make the next gate. But something like this will usually only happen on the right at the start of your first practice day. After that you adjust yourself accordingly and drive slower at a particular point so as not to miss the right 'exit' next time. But here too it is a matter of the right speed, and not the choice of any ideal line as such. This line virtually draws itself and everybody drives the same line. Anybody who cannot find it easily just does not have what it takes to be a racing driver, let alone a Formula I performer.

THE TEN TOUGHEST BENDS

So as not to go too much into pure theory, I will describe the various kinds of cornering using various examples in real race tracks, the ten Grand Prix bends that I myself regard as the toughest or most interesting examples. As elsewhere in this book I am talking only about the Formula I – an ordinary motorist would probably look at them quite differently. I deal with them in alphabetical order.

Barcelona (Montjuich Park)

I come flat out into the start and finishing straight, and get maximum revs in fifth gear. At this point I am batting down towards a hump, and keep my foot on the gas until just before the car lifts off. Right after the touchdown I have to tread on the brakes to be ready for the second-gear left-hand bend coming up. The whole business is complicated by the fact that the hump is on a shallow curve. While I do my best to come up to it on the outside so I can take it in a straight line I still cannot leave the ground squarely which means I do not land squarely either – I probably land first on my right front wheel. This crooked touchdown causes the car to swing about, and then right in the middle of that I have got to tread on the brakes. It takes a lot of nerve to keep up the power until the very last moment because: the faster I am on take-off, the further the car will jump; and the longer that jump the less braking distance I will have for the following dead-slow left hand bend. On practice laps I come up to

What I personally regard as one of the ten toughest bends on today's Grand Prix tracks: the sharp left plus hump at Barcelona. In this photo is Jochen Mass, victor of the 1975 race that was so tragically broken off.

that hump at first with marked respect, I take my foot off the gas and try out the various ways of taking it. Then I tinker about with the car for a while and try to get as close as possible to the optimum set-up that will allow me to take the hump flat out (the problem being not the leap itself but the reduced braking distance after it).

This stretch is particularly piquant for this reason: the long straight before the hump offers the only real place for overtaking people on the entire track. If the car I am overtaking pulls to the inside on the hump (and they usually do) then he forces me to take off on the outside and virtually conclude the over-

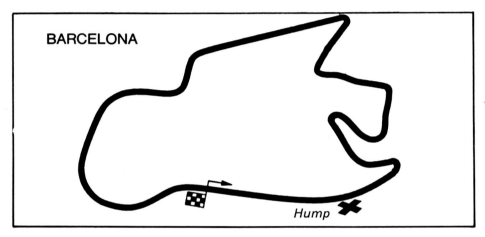

taking manoeuvre in mid-air, as well as touching down on his outside too. But on the outside I obviously cannot keep take off and landing in one straight line so it is even less square than normally and I find myself fighting with the car's swinging even more afterwards – in short it is a particularly insidious and difficult place. I really have to force myself every time to keep my foot on the accelerator. But when all is said and done I believe I really do like this spot because it is one of the few places that show up the true differences between drivers.

Brands Hatch

Brands Hatch is a special case among all the world's Grand Prix tracks. It is the most difficult and unpleasant track, because the road surface is irregular virtually throughout. Your car never stops jumping about. The more wing we apply, the more the car is pressed towards the ground and the more it hits the bump stops of the suspension, which only causes it to leap about the more. So when we set the wings we have to go for a compromise.

On account of Brands Hatch's special nature I am going to describe two bends there. Let us take Clearways first, a right hand bend before the starting and finishing line. Right in the middle of the bend the asphalt suddenly changes, and the track banks to the outside. You can imagine what then happens: the car begins to slither outwards in the most hair-raising way. Even when I was driving Formula III's I was wide awake to the dangers of this bend but I still managed to get flung out of a Formula III race there in a spectacular manner.

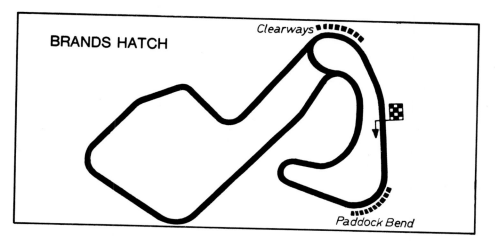

Paddock Bend, the right hand bend following the starting and finishing line, is no easy meat either. It is a downhill bend that is relatively broad, banks outwards and then narrows off. If you go into it flat out you suddenly run out of track, you find you are on the outside – but you must not get too far out, because if you do you will not be able to get back in; and you have to hit just the right speed to understeer slightly, because the exit from the bend has adverse camber. Even braking into Paddock Bend is a nasty experience, because the braking surface there is enormously bumpy. You arrive in fourth gear and take the bend in third.

Interlagos

Every time you take the 'Curva 2' here it is a trial of courage; you can never say this bend ever becomes routine, you have to take your courage in both hands every time. We employ, of course, a fifth-gear ratio at Interlagos that

Paddock Bend at Brands Hatch: above, the starting bunch in the 1974 Grand Prix; below the scene in the 1974 Race of Champions in which I just outbrake Emerson Fittipaldi before Paddock Bend – in pouring rain.

will just give me top revs at the end of the long straight (i.e., just before Curva 3). You are only making a few hundred revs less at the end of the starting straight, i.e., just before Curva 1, and it is here that the test of nerves begins. In the Ferrari, I arrive there in fifth gear with 12,000 rpm. Normally I just hit the brakes hard once, then I find out in the practice laps that I can take it faster and faster through that bend, and then the moment comes when I take the plunge and risk it flat out, without even braking – in fifth gear, just briefly lifting my foot off the accelerator pedal. In other words : foot quickly off, throw the wheel over (it's downhill slightly), then foot hard down, and this carries me automatically right to the outer edge of the track. But at this moment the

Another view of Paddock Bend, with Regazzoni leading Peterson (1974 Grand Prix).

125

next left hand bend begins, and that is the Curva 2. Now, if you are driving a perfect car and know your stuff you will keep your foot on the gas right through this second bend and when you come out of it you will be in full drift. In fifth gear you slither right over to the outer edge, where there is a narrow elevated strip with the guard rail behind it – and behind that is a narrow concrete tower that gets bigger and bigger and bigger as you drift outwards towards it . . . and it takes the whole of the straight after that to calm down again and for the three times after that you take your foot *off* the gas until you can once again force yourself to keep it on. Obviously you are only going to take this risk if you have got a really great car, because when you are drifting with your foot hard on the gas you have no room for error – the slightest slip and you are out. This bend is one of the few places in the world where you can see Formula I cars drifting flat out in fifth gear. If your car is strongly understeering then you have no option but to take your foot off the gas and wait until your nose points back in, then you can put the foot down again. If the understeering is only slight, then I am obliged to decelerate slightly at the apex of Curva 2, then accelerate again to push out the rear of the car, so I start drifting properly. But as said if all the conditions are right you can take the entire stretch from the starting line right round to the long straight with your foot hard down (apart from a small easing of the accelerator just before Curva 1), taking it all in one smooth radius without any sharp corners. The centrifugal force is in fact so strong that you will have difficulty keeping your helmet on straight. Interlagos is the only Grand Prix track in the world that leaves me with neck pains for

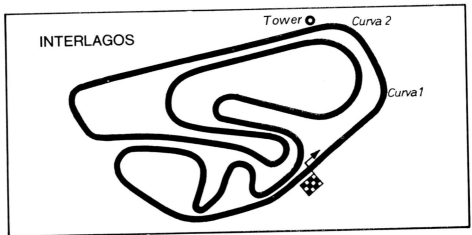

two days afterwards. Once I found myself doing exercises two weeks before the races to strengthen my neck muscles. Some drivers have had elastic reins installed, running from the car's bodywork to their crash helmet, to help them keep their head and helmet upright. Be that as it may, if you want to see Formula I cars drifting magnificently in fifth gear, then you must come to Brazil and stand by the Curva 2 at Interlagos.

Monza

The Curva Grande is a long, easy right-hand bend at the end of the start-and-finish straight. In earlier years, before they built the chicane, the Curva Grande was a real problem. You used to accelerate fast out of the Parabolica, hit top speed on the long straight and then the Curva Grande. But now they have built a second-gear chicane right after the starting line so that you hit the Grande at a much lower speed. It is still quite an interesting problem, but since that chicane's installation it does not really count as one of the most exciting

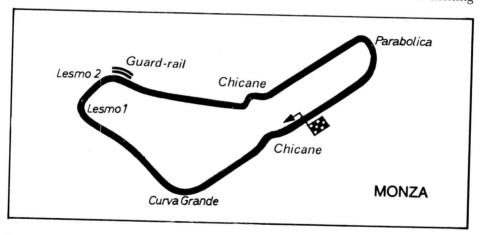

bends in the world. Among them however I would list the two-Lesmo combination, where the guard-rails are lying in wait for you right after you leave the bend. Lesmo 1 is a right-hand bend for third gear, then you select fourth and enter Lesmo 2 which is absolutely vital because it is out of this curve that you accelerate into a long straight. If you fumble Lesmo 2 you will lose a lot of time on the straight. In the endeavour to take Lesmo 2 as fast as possible you allow your car to go right over to the edge – risking inching right up to the guard-rail that sprouts all along it. Twice on practice laps I have just slightly touched that rail with my rear : afterwards I naturally had to have the car's geometry checked to see that everything was still okay. In the actual race, if you are really battling for position and let yourself go you find yourself slithering towards that guard-rail and steel yourself for the crunch : ouch, here it comes.

Mosport (Canada)

At that part of the track that is furthest from the start and finish line a particular hazard – and another trial of courage – lies in wait for you. This is the approach to the sharp-about-turn (second gear). Before this hairpin bend there is a flat-out shallow left-hand curve that drops down into a depression, then climbs again to the about-turn. If you want to get anywhere at Mosport, then you are going to have to take that shallow left without easing your foot off the accelerator one bit. The problem is, that the actual surface is convex, so you cannot see where you are going at all : you find yourself diving down into that depression without seeing a thing. Driving downhill, on a sharply banked road, you then have to brake into that hairpin bend – and that means a drop in speed of just over 60 mph. You then have to try to carry the car through the conflicting forces and trends of this about-turn in such a way that you do not emerge from it at an angle, thus ending up in the braking zone. And all the time you are trying to cope with this, there is the added refinement that you are careering downhill and cannot see where you are going.

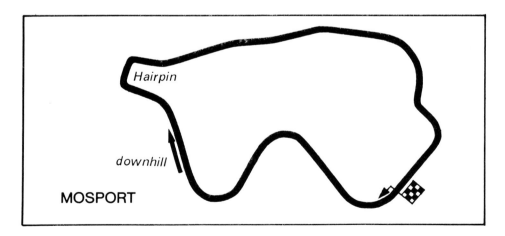

Nürburgring

The spot where I had my bad accident in 1976 is not interesting at all – it is one of the most boring places for the spectators.

But there is one other part that I regard as the most exciting place in all the world's Grand Prix tracks, in other words even tougher and more fascinating than the Curva 2 at Interlagos. This is the last surviving full-blown take-off hump, which once caused Stuck to say: 'That knocks the wind out of you down to the last fart!' You will find it between Pflanzgarten and the Swallowtail, in other words after about three-quarters of the Nordschleife. The whole thing hits you faster than you can think: you come at it flat out and have to react like lightning to completely different situations. The first thing is, you have to try to hit the hump as square as possible. So you have to haul well out at *A* in order to come right over to the inside at *B*, the only way of hitting the hump even approximately straight. You never pull it off one hundred per cent, you always take off a bit askew and land even more crooked. The first wheel to touch

Between the Pflanzgarten and the Swallowtail with all four wheels in the air.

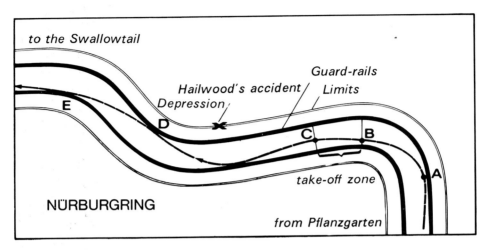

to the Swallowtail

Guard-rails

Hailwood's accident / *Limits*

Depression

E

D

C

B

A

take-off zone

NÜRBURGRING

from Pflanzgarten

down (at *C*) is your right front wheel, and if you have done it well you will be on the left of the track centre so as to be well positioned for *D*.

Before all this you will just have changed up from fourth to fifth gear; at *A* you are right on the outside, trying to line up your car squarely so as to take *B* and the hump behind it in one straight line. If I square up to *B* badly, I will be too far to the right on take off and landing and I will not get back to the left soon enough to be in the right position to line up for *D*. And if I do not take *D* right then I am going to get into difficulties at *E* – in other words all this means that between *A* and *B* I am laying the foundations for a stretch of nearly a mile of track : that's the choice – either fast, slow or leave the track. All this is dramatic enough, but it becomes an even bigger headache when the problem of the touchdown itself is considered.

As there is just no way of taking off squarely, you are going to touch down crooked whatever you do. You are going to land on your right front wheel, so you will have your hands full to prevent the car leaving the track. It looks worst of all with production-line cars – they take the whole road width and swerve from side to side. But even Formula I cars begin swerving sideways most unpleasantly. To bring this under control before you reach *D* is the art that has to be mastered here. The ideal case looks like this : you touch down,

The late Carlos Pace showing us how to take-off (1974). He has come squarely over the hump and is on the proper left hand side, well positioned to take the coming twist. Note the slight listing of the car to the right: the car is going to touch down first with its right front wheel.

swerve to the right, correct to the left and just manage to wriggle past D with the resulting swerve to the right. If you cannot coax this initial right-hand swerve out of your car on touch down – i.e., if it goes left instead – then you are going to have to brake and lose time; the alternative is to shoot off the track. There is one particular refinement here : if you are not spot on at D you may hit the curb, which is a real right-angle just there. Your car will get such a box on the ears then that you will still be fighting with it at E and taking the curb there in your stride as well . . . and then you really are in a crisis situation.

Of course you may well write yourself off even before then, right after touch down. That was how Mike Hailwood had the bad accident that put an end to his career in 1974 : his right wheel made such a bad landing that it jerked the whole car to the right and hurled him into the guard-rail at right-angles.

To sum up : you have to deal with three problems virtually all at the same time. The right line, so as to take off squarely; the right landing, with its subsequent swerving; and avoiding the curbstones. Of course the drama only begins when you are driving flat out. You can always brake and funnel your car through without much difficulty.

Zeltweg

I am not thinking here of the Bosch Bend with its attendant guard-rail acrobatics but of the almost inconspicuous up hill right-hand bend after the start-and finishing line : this is the Hella Light Bend. The problems here are your fantastic speed – you will only just have reached maximum revs in fifth gear – and the fact that as you come up hill you cannot see the exit from the bend. So you get no help whatever in deciding just when to throw the wheel over. Not until you are actually over the brow of the hill do you find out whether you have taken it right or wrong. If you have begun cornering too soon, you find yourself on the very nasty cobblestones that make up the shoulder of the track; if you have thrown the wheel over to the right too late, you will not make the exit from that bend and you will wind up in the guard-rail. Of course it depends how you have set up your car : if I have put on a lot of wing I can sail through it; but if I have set up the car for top speeds – which is in fact the best thing for this track – the bend is a nasty blighter. It is one of those places where you get no second chance : woe betide you if you begin to slide. That's why you have got to put your foot hard down, hard, hard, and tell yourself each time anew that that's the only way to take it.

132

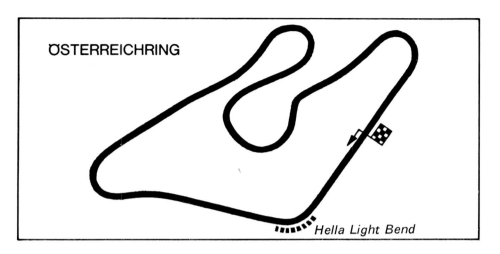

ÖSTERREICHRING

Hella Light Bend

This photo gives a clear picture of what the driver sees — or rather, cannot see — as he comes up to the Hella Light Bend: 'You get no help whatever in deciding just when to throw the wheel over. . . .'

Seen from above, the Hella Light Bend does not look nearly so dramatic. But the cars' speed as they take this right hand bend is usually so high that they cannot afford to make errors.

Silverstone

Woodcote used to be one of the classic bends, and that is why I include it here although it has since been 'defused' by the introduction of a chicane. It was the fast right-hand bend just before the start and finishing-line. The entry into the bend had a very wide track, but at its exit – just before the start and finishing-line – the track was relatively narrow. After a while you took Woodcote Bend in fifth gear with just a gentle easing of the accelerator: admittedly it took some practice getting it just right – you used to start off by taking it in fourth gear. If you were in dead earnest you took it in fifth, eased slightly, had to hit the entry bang-on and then you ran over a nasty bump in the middle of the bend and that made your car jump about a bit. After that you had the exit from the bend – much too narrow for your liking – and with a jumpy car on top of all that. Once you were past the apex there was practically nothing more you could do: you put your foot hard down and just hoped for the best. And if the worse came to the worst you ended up with what happened to Jody Scheckter in 1973 in the first lap: he carried on too far, ran onto the grass, spun round, shot back across the track and crashed into the pit wall. That caused the famous mass pile-up.

134

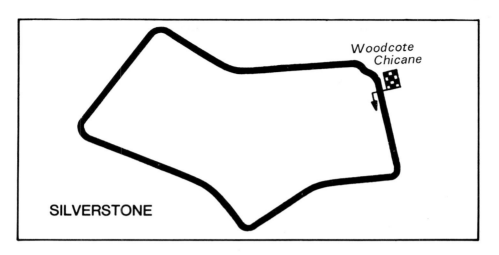

Woodcote Bend after the mass pile-up in 1973.

Watkins Glen

The most difficult stretch here is the one that proved fatal to François Cevert:
at the bridge about a mile after the start. After the starting straight you take
an easy right-hand bend, followed by a right-left curve that takes you over a
bridge, after which you hit the long straight. To get the best possible acceleration into that straight, you have got to pass that bridge spot on. By 'bridge', I
mean that here the guard-rails come almost right to the edge of the track so you
have not even the slightest room for play. What matters is the slight left-hand
curve before the bridge; but let us begin with the right-hander before that.
Going into this right-hander you change from outside to inside lane. In normal

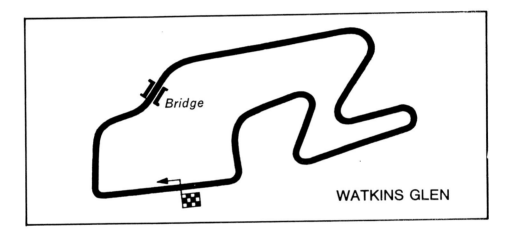

circumstances you would then be forced over to the outside again but this
would leave you no room to take that bridge. So you have got to try to come
out of that right-hander in the middle of the track, so as to have your hands
free as you go into the left-hander. On this left-hander the curbs are extremely
dangerous – if you touch them it can be fatal. Eye-witnesses of the Cevert crash
say that François took it just a shade too far to the west, brushed one curb and
took such a knock that his car moved too far to the right on the bridge, his two
right wheels came in contact with the guard-rail, the car began to spin, swerved
right across the track and hit the other guard-rail almost head-on. I saw myself

Driving up to the notorious 'bridge' at Watkins Glen, in the USA Grand Prix of 1974 (Reutemann, Hunt, myself, Regazzoni, Fittipaldi, Watson): after leaving the right-hand bend you must try to hit the middle of the track.

how the whole monocoque became wedged under the guard-rail—it had uprooted the supports and bent the rail up, leaving only the rear wheels still on the track.

Zandvoort

I do not want to leave out the notorious Tarzan Bend, which runs from Scheivlak *A* to the chicane subsequently installed at *B*. If you want to win, then you are going to have to take the whole stretch flat out: first a left-hand curve, then a right-hand one, then another right-hander, followed by the chicane. The radii of each of these curves is such that you can just take them flat out, which means you will not have another ounce of power if you hit a snag. The result is that for a thousand yards you find yourself tightrope walking at maximum revs.

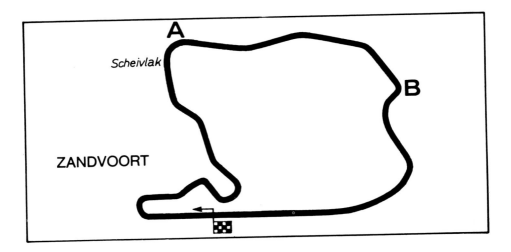

Tests and Training

When I am doing testing, my daily routine is nothing like that of the other Grand Prix drivers, for the simple reason that of all the Formula I racing stables, only Ferrari offers the kind of opportunities that they do. Only Ferrari have their own works racetrack, and it is only three minutes away from the factory. Only Ferrari has that bank of optical and electronic measuring and control devices. Thus there are photoelectric beams permanently built into the track both before and at all critical points along the 2,990 metre test stretch, in addition to which the car is followed by ten television cameras, also permanently installed. So we can follow every lap without a break on the TV monitors, and of course we can record it and store it, so the driver can analyse his own driving later on. The photoelectric cell data is automatically computed, so we get all the facts we need to know about the various intervals and velocities just by reading the print-out. What makes these print-outs so interesting is that they enable us to analyse in detail the result of every adjustment we make to the car: we can say, for instance, this or that one has proved its value on fast bends, it does this or that on the straight, it is good or bad for winding stretches and so on. By adding chicanes it is possible to simulate conditions just as they are on real tracks.

Once you have made the acquaintance of these absolutely first class working conditions and you realize what they are worth, you just cannot imagine ever working for another company that just rents a test track now and again to test drive its cars. So in this respect we are head and shoulders above the rest.

What is equally important is that Fiorano is also a track of exemplary safety, so you can carry out test drives with a minimum of risk. The run-off areas are very spacious and there are no solid obstacles apart from a single crossbridge.

Whenever any car is being driven at racing speed there, three men are always on duty, and a fire tender and ambulance stand by with engines running. One

Starting-and-finishing straight of Ferrari's Fiorano test track at Maranello. The display board automatically registers the last lap time recorded. At 1 minute 12.83 seconds the lap shown here was 1.10 seconds slower than my own lap record. The Ferrari big noises standing at the table are (left to right) Enzo Ferrari's (illegitimate) son Piero Lardi, his organiser Ghedini, development chief Forghieri and technician Tomaini.

TV monitor room at the Fiorano test track. During each lap the car is followed by TV cameras all the time. The computer on the left spews out the printed-out photoelectric cell readings.

fireman is also already standing by dressed in an asbestos suit – and that is always, absolutely always. Unless these precautions have been taken it is flatly forbidden to drive even one lap there.

Here at Maranello we make a distinction between three different kinds of tests :

○ the weeks of testing before a completely new car design is sent racing;
○ tests of new component designs;
○ routine test on whatever actual car and practice cars are being used for a race meeting, a few days beforehand.

Other testing is of course done apart from that at Fiorano, virtually always in conjunction with the tyre company (which nowadays means Goodyear) and virtually always in conjunction with other first-class teams. These practice laps are done more or less in public, a few weeks before a Grand Prix and on the racing track concerned. This is when the precise combination of tyres, car and track is perfected.

Here I am demonstrating understeering and oversteering with one and the same car on two different bends of our test track at Fiorano. For these photographs I deliberately had the anti-roll bars and wings wrongly set, because although you can – with a bit of effort – demonstrate oversteering with a neutrally adjusted Formula I car, you cannot simulate understeering. The upper photograph (oversteering) demonstrates how much opposite lock you have to apply to the steering wheel just in order to keep the car on the road. It is not possible to drive exactly on the line you want, nor can I accelerate cleanly out of the bend because if I do then the car will just oversteer even more. In the lower photograph (understeering) we can see how reluctant the car is to follow the front wheels round the bend, but keeps trying to move outwards. Here too it is difficult to drive an ideal line, because your car will only react weakly to steering corrections.

TEST WEEKS

Let us look first at a situation that only crops up once every few years : the birth of a completely new car design. I had the great fortune to be with Ferrari when the 312 T was finding its feet – it was not without a certain excitement and fascination to be the first man on earth to be allowed to drive this car. And it meant even more to me perhaps to be allowed to influence the car's design right from the start.

In such tests your first job is always getting the feel of the new car. The first thing is to install springs just on the basis of experience and to drive the first laps just so as to get some kind of picture of the car. These first laps are usually interrupted by minor defects like leaking oil, water or fuel connections, or faulty gear changes. Only when all these minor defects have been overcome can you really begin driving properly and marking up the first timed laps. Then you alter and adjust the springing and the anti-roll bars in both directions – harder or softer, depending primarily on the lap times recorded but also on the car's road handling (it is no use cutting one or two tenths of a second off a lap if the car reacts like poison and you are teetering on the brink of destruction the whole time). The result then will be very widely differing lap times, because you will easily make driving errors.

The test programme then continues with various alterations to the castor angle[1] of the front axle, again in both directions, and to the toe-in[2] both front and rear. In addition to various ride heights the various aerodynamic aids are also tried out – in short everything necessary to get the feel of the car and its character.

But all this is only possible if you drive several laps after every adjustment –

[1] You can witness the effect of the castor-angle best from supermarket trolleys, dinner wagons, and wheelchairs. The wheels are suspended in a fork that pivots in a vertical socket, and are thus trailed along. The distance between the tyre's contact point and the projection of the centre of the socket – or in a racing car, the projection of the line joining the ball sockets at the outer end of the wishbones – is the 'castor angle'; it is a matter of only a few millimetres. The more this distance, the greater are the opposing forces when the car corners, in other words the car is hard to steer. If the distance is too small, however, while the car is easy to steer you lose 'feeling' – the driver does not feel enough car reaction to his steering wheel. The castor angle can be adjusted by displacing the wishbones.
[2] The two wheels on one axle are not truly parallel to each other, but converge in an angle too small for the eye to perceive – normally about half of one degree in the front, and five or ten minutes of a degree in the rear. This 'toe-in' helps stabilize the car, particularly when braking, and prevents the wheels fluttering. It can be adjusted by lengthening or shortening the track rods (in front) and the radius rods and wishbones (in the rear).

In all thoroughbred racing engines throttle-slides are used, not butterflies. The slides, usually made of aluminium, are moved in the throttle housing by corresponding accelerator pedal movements. This picture shows the slide serving the left hand cylinder block; it is almost closed, so the engine would just tick over. To minimize the foot pressure necessary to operate the slide, it is mounted on roller bearings. This picture shows the earlier (1972) version of the Ferrari 12-cylinder engine, as is apparent from two details: the combined injection pump and ignition unit is still mounted on the engine's front end; it was later moved on top, to reduce the engine's length. And the injection jets are here still in the induction channel behind the slide; 1977 engines have them in the induction trumpets as this results in better cooling of the inducted air.

and at your best possible speed. I can only go on to a new adjustment when all the fastest laps are exactly the same to the nearest tenth of a second. A typical sequence of lap times would then look something like this : 1 : 15.0 − 1 : 14.0 − 1 : 13.9 − 1 : 13.9 − 1 : 13.7 − 1 : 13.6 − 1 : 13.6 − 1 : 13.6. Then I can stop and proceed to the next variation. If I commit a minor driving slip on one of these laps, that lap obviously does not 'count' and I have to repeat it.

Driving fast like that it often happens that you just drive right past a problem, so to speak : you are so preoccupied with the actual driving that you may not even notice other problems arising, perhaps brand new ones. But you can teach yourself to make time to take in all such aspects and pay proper attention to them.

There are many adjustments where the lap times alone do not tell you enough, they still leave you in some doubt. What is then absolutely vital is to undertake so-called 'repeats' − to restore the car to an earlier state and test again from there. You may well find yourself dismantling, adjusting, dismantling and re-adjusting two or three times. Of course there is no need for this if a particular modification cuts say three clear tenths off your lap time.

TEST ROUTINE

The procedure is similar, though on a smaller scale, if new components need to be tried out during the racing season. The spectrum of such components ranges from airboxes to the different possible cooling ducts. You never get bored, if you as the driver can do your share of the thinking and do not just have to stamp on the pedal, but can do your own bit towards helping each different modification.

After that, somebody also has to check each race car and training car before they are loaded on to the transporter. This time is also used for running in a stock of brake-pads. On days like these all the safety measures are still in force at Fiorano − for every car there are four mechanics on the track, the technicians and managers are there . . . . so the cost is not inconsiderable.

TYRE TESTS

Among these are above all the test days organized by Goodyear on the various tracks. Most of the teams and all the best drivers take part in them − it is all just like a Grand Prix, but the spectators' stands are empty. Whatever the innovations being tested, they are all rounded up and called in afterwards . . .

The wing adjustment has a big influence on a car's handling. As the car is very sensitive to this adjustment, the wing angle is very finely set with the help of a combined spirit level and protractor. By using different combinations of bolt-holes in the two wing supports it is possible to make whatever adjustments are needed.

*Two mechanics adjust the measuring device used mainly on the race tracks.
The two sets of verticals (shown here pushed together, for setting-up purposes)
are brought into close contact with the wheel rims: this enables them to make a
quick check on the wheels' toe-in.*

and come the next race meeting all the teams are back on the same kind of tyres again.

Ferrari is able of course to carry out tyre tests at its own expense at Fiorano. What is important in any tyre test, is that you have to keep on fitting a 'control set' of normal tyres so as to check whether the factors assumed at the beginning of the test (factors relating to the car, the weather and road surface) are remaining constant.

DEFECTS

It is in the nature of the sport that all these tests and all the outlay described can only help to reduce the number of defects but that there will never be a complete Grand Prix season without some incident or other occurring. There will always be new sudden crises that you can not predict or simulate completely during trials.

Of course every defect is subjected to intensive analysis, and a convincing explanation is almost always found for it so that precautions can be taken against it in time for the next race. My own list of defects detected over the last three years will give an example of what things are like in practice, and what we can learn from them :

1974:
O   Buenos Aires : no defect – second place.
O   Interlagos : a new engine was installed for the race. One of the 96 valve springs broke at the start, which brought the race to an abrupt end for me. The manufacturer's detailed analysis showed there was a material defect in the production of the valve-spring steel. In a case like this a specialist of the firm concerned will immediately visit Ferrari's to make sure the valve-spring's pre-tensioning (its installation-length) is correct. If the outcome is that the defective spring is one of a batch that has already caused a problem elsewhere, then all the springs of this batch are withdrawn from use.
O   Kyalami : two laps from the end the engine began missing, first at 12,300 rpm then at lower and lower revs until it stopped altogether. Diagnosis : a defect in the transistorized ignition circuit. The ignition was thoroughly checked by Magneti Marelli, but they could not find any fault in it. It was returned to Ferrari's and by mistake installed in my car all over again, in time for Monte Carlo.
O   Jarama : won without problems, although the drive cable of my rev counter snapped. As I was not being forced to drive under pressure, it was no real

148

loss – I was able to change gear with enough revs in hand. Of course, you know all the gear-change points along the track, including those for changing-up. If the rev counter breaks down then you just change gear a bit before these points (if you are changing up) or a bit after (if changing down). To take the car up to the rev limiter's pre-set limit is not advisable, because you can never be quite sure that the limiter is working precisely (it is a very tricky device).

○ Monaco : see Kyalami. I was way out in front after thirty laps, when my ignition began misfiring, worse and worse until the engine died completely. After the race the engine started perfectly again. On the following Monday we took the car to Dijon immediately. Six engineers from Magneti Marelli watched the tests on it for two days. Although the conditions were virtually the same as at Monte Carlo, the defect did not display itself. To be on the safe side the defective ignition system was scrapped. After that we had no more problems of misfiring.

○ Nivelles : second place after Fittipaldi, no defects. It just wasn't possible to get past Fittipaldi.

○ Zandvoort : victory, no problems.

○ Dijon : during the race one tyre took on an oval shape. Because of the powerful vibrations that were set up I had to let Peterson pass me, and I came second. Afterwards Goodyear discovered a manufacturing defect (uneven rubber thickness). It is the only defect of this kind I ever heard of.

○ Brands Hatch : tyre damage on right rear wheel when I was lying in front a few laps before the finish. With a slow puncture you are faced with the decision whether to carry on to the finish or head for the pits : the decision is not easy, and luck plays a part in it. I decided to carry on, still had to make for the pits however and found myself in the familiar pits turmoil just before the end of the race : fifth place.

○ Nürburgring : an accident, my own fault thanks to curious circumstances – see below under 'My Worst Start'.

○ Zeltweg : yet another valve spring broke. Engine lacked performance right from the start, then died on me.

○ Monza : leaking water hose – loss of water – engine-damage. Analysis : the connection to the water pump was faulty on account of a crossed thread. The engine assembly section is responsible for this connection, in other words the men who prepare the engine at Maranello for racing. When the engine is installed into the car (on the actual track) we therefore pay no attention to this detail. Because of the crossed thread and the vibrations

Pile-up at the start of Barcelona 1975. The movie camera began rolling just a fraction of a second too late: the cause of the crash is visible only on the second and third photographs (the damaged right front wing of Mario Andretti's car No. 27). After getting that shunt I found myself ploughing out of control into the guard rail, and there I collided with Regazzoni.

during the race the fastening ring worked loose and water began leaking out. Cure : the fastening ring is now secured with wire.

○ Mosport : skidded off the track while in the lead (I hit a patch of sand thrown up by Watson in front of me, as I was just about to lap him). I was so close behind him that the track officials were not able to warn me in time – and on loose sand it is like driving on ice.

○ Watkins Glen : Shock absorber damaged after a valve broke in the shock absorber's seating.

1975:

○ Buenos Aires : during the race a tyre on one side wore out unusually fast because during its manufacture they had left out one layer of rubber on its inside edge by mistake. The car began to oversteer more and more in consequence because the tyre had only 200 millimetres of tread-width left. I just managed to scrape into sixth place.

○ Interlagos : warming up on the morning of the race, the engine went. As there was not enough time left for a complete engine change, we transferred the entire rear end of the mule (including the engine and gearbox) to the monocoque of the race car. In other words I was driving two cars at the same time, with results that suffered accordingly. Came fifth.

○ Kyalami : first time using the T-model Ferrari. The advantages of the new car were already making themselves felt, when the ignition/injection timing began to shift during the actual race. On the test rig afterwards we found that the engine was developing about 85 horsepower less than it should. Came fifth.

○ Monte Carlo : Victory, with knocking knees! During the race the engine started consuming too much oil (because of a leaky oil seal on the mechanical fuel pump; on some bends I was getting no oil pressure at all. At first I said in interviews that it was just the oil warning lamp flickering – perhaps because of a loose contact. As nobody thought of asking if I did not check the oil pressure reading, I did not have to think up any further explanations. But I could tell the engine was close to the end from its vibrations : that could only mean that the main bearings were about to go. In fact on some of the bends on the last two laps I actually declutched, so as to spare the engine. This was why Fittipaldi got so close to me at the finish. One more lap and he would have had me.

○ Barcelona : my crash overshadowed this race – Andretti gave me a shunt in the rear at the start (see photos on page 150-1).

152

○ Zolder : an exhaust tail pipe broke off, otherwise no problems. I was able to put up with the 300 rpm this cost me on the straight as my own lead was already big enough. Victory.

○ Anderstorp : no problem with the car, chose the proper tyres – the harder ones. Victory.

○ Zandvoort : second to James Hunt. No problem with the car, which had been set up to get the best out of a wet day. As a result I was able to pull ahead right from the start. Whether my late tyre change made any difference I cannot say. To take account of the rainy surface I had put on a lot of wing, which gave Hunt an advantage over me on the straight – i.e., the only place where you could overtake.

○ Paul Ricard : no problems. I managed to put myself across the finishing line before James Hunt, with a bit of effort on my part.

○ Silverstone : a front wheel not properly tightened up after a tyre change cost me the race. A nightmare situation that I would like to forget as soon as possible. The thread was repaired as a lightning job in time for the next race.

1976:

○ Interlagos : victory after hard work, but no other problems.

○ Kyalami : on the 20th lap the car suddenly began pulling to the left, driving it was murder, it just was not possible to put on a 'well rounded, progressive' performance. Cause was a slow puncture in the left rear tyre – slowly but infuriatingly surely the air leaked out. As though that was not enough the brakes also gave me a headache : on the practice laps I had adjusted the brakes distribution so that the front wheels slightly overbraked. Probably because of some temperature effect, this now changed to precisely the reverse so that the rear wheels braked stronger. It was maddening. Every couple of laps or so I had virtually to get used to a completely different car – every couple of laps I had to work out a new line.

Hunt noticed of course that I had hit problems and that was just about the best moral tonic he could have hoped for, and he hounded me pitilessly. Just before the last lap fortune played into my hands a little – fortune in the person of John Watson. On the long straight he was in front of me and I knew : You've got to overtake him and then brake whatever happens, so as to put him between Hunt and your car. This hair-raising manoeuvre came off, and victory was mine.

○ Long Beach : I hit a lot of snags on the practice laps, and I was racing on the defensive behind Regazzoni in second place. Fifteen laps before the end I began hearing alarming noises that remained constant whatever the engine revs – which meant they were coming from the gearbox, not the engine. I immediately slowed down by 3 or 4 seconds per lap and took even the hairpin bends in second gear, and only put my foot half on the gas – I just about managed to finish.

○ Jarama : I had been in a nasty tractor accident and damaged several ribs, so I had to drive carefully here. I was happy enough to come second to Hunt.

○ Zolder : I was lying well out in front when my car suddenly began over-steering 20 laps from the finish. I assumed that the tyre or suspension had bought it, and was about to head for the pits, but instead I drove on care-fully for a few laps and noticed oil contaminating the first three bends that I had not seen before. I managed to come first after all.

○ Monaco : victory after a lot of hard work, but no technical snags.

○ Anderstorp : one of the few races in recent years in which Ferrari just did not manage to match their cars to the performance of the competition : our cars were simply not as good as the Tyrrells, which meant here was nothing I could do against Scheckter and Depailler. Came third.

○ Le Castellet : an extremely rare defect for a Ferrari – I had snatched the lead very early on and then, bang in the middle of the Mistral straight the terrifying thing happened right out of the blue : sudden silence, and my rear wheels locked. The Ferrari spun out of control and ran right across the track. I don't think I've ever stamped on a clutch so fast in my life before. As Regazzoni's engine also seized up in this race we realized that our attempts to squeeze a few more horsepower out of the engines had over-done it, for the time being.

○ Brands Hatch : there is little to be said on the technical aspects of this race. The race was stopped after a collision : Hunt went back to the re-start – which was a breach of the rules, as he should have completed the lap first. He won, but the point was later awarded to me.

○ Nürburgring : there's not much I can say about this, the worst crash in my racing life, as I suffered total amnesia about the event and twenty minutes after. Later on I often saw the film showing how the crash happened, but I never have found out why my Ferrari suddenly swerved to the right.

○ Monza : this was the first race after my recovery, and I did what I could. On the last lap the oil pressure dropped and I took my foot off the gas a bit, as I wanted to finish at all costs. In the circumstances, fourth place was not bad at all for me.

○ Mosport: cold weather brought out one of the Ferrari's weaknesses. When the camber of a wheel changes dramatically as it raises or droops on its suspension, it causes heat in the tyres; and the ideal temperature of a racing tyre is a little over 100 degrees C. The cars of most teams have suspensions that do a lot of work, while the play in our cars is almost nil. In consequence, when the days were hot we had the advantage: but at Mosport it worked against us. After a very tricky get-away, a rear wheel suspension component snapped and threw me right back. Came eighth.

○ Watkins Glen: basically the same dilemma as at Mosport. Towards the end the car scarcely manageable. Logically enough, it was okay at the beginning (after all I had 44 gallons of petrol aboard, putting a useful extra load on the tyres). But the lighter my car became the more critical the tyre adhesion, as they just never reached their optimum working temperature. All in all, I had to be pleased that I came third.

○ Fuji: I comment fully on my decision to quit this rain race, later in this book. From a purely technical point of view there are of course many ways of driving Formula I cars even in heavy rain. It would call for a different rain tyre, with about two inches of tread depth and much narrower dimensions. I do not think much of adding mudguards to Formula I cars – I still think my decision then was the right one, although it cost me the world championship: today's cars and tyres were not designed to drive in the kind of conditions there were that day at Fuji.

TRAINING

The test drives about five days before each race in order to check over the car that is to be used are a matter of course for Ferrari, but *only* for Ferrari while the other teams have to do without them as they have no test track. What this means is that Ferrari drivers are able to use every minute of the official practice time, because the cars unloaded from their transporters are already in tip-top condition: you won't find for instance that this or that pipeline is leaking.

Of course, I will already have done some thinking about the various gear ratios and other adjustments that I want to be made. The sooner the car is 'set up', the sooner you can get down to the real job in hand – driving the fastest possible laps, particularly when you are wrestling for the pole position.

POLE POSITION

Why the pole position is so vital, and why a place in the third row in the grid is so much better than one in the sixth, is obvious from the fact that the cars are so identical: since they are all virtually equally fast overtaking is a real struggle (at Barcelona and Monza it is almost impossible). The more cars you don't have to overtake because you're already so far in front at the start, the better. A really good driver will not get his best time by chance, so his fastest lap is not going to be just one of many laps. You have to draw a clear distinction between routine laps and the fight for the fastest lap, which is of course only worthwhile after all the adjustments have been made to the car (and with many teams these adjustments are never really completed, so you may find yourself racing with an unsatisfying car). But assuming that everything has gone marvellously and the car is 'right', then you have got to start thinking about how you are going to drive it. You will have got a rough idea anyway – your target will either be the first or the second day. Monaco for instance is a relatively clean surface that gets visibly worse (because there are Formula III cars practising too, and a lot of oil and rubber debris) – so you will as a rule drive faster laps on the first day than on the second. On most of the permanent race tracks precisely the reverse is the case: the second day is usually faster there, because the fine film of sand and dust covering the surface is slipstreamed off during the first practice day. That all such thoughts come to naught anyway if the weather dramatically changes is of course obvious.

When the time comes I am fully genned up as to the previous lap times – both my own and my rivals'. What I now have to do is try slicing tenths of a second off my times: on a track of average length your target will be a reduction of

In mid 1975 Ferrari began tests with the De-Dion rear suspension. Gone is the massive De-Dion tube of the good old days, but this design still has the desired effects: the rear wheels have the same track and camber whatever the car's attitude. The solution shown here is a purely strut-design which puts the individual components only under tension and compression. It has the added advantage that the amount of toe-in can be easily adjusted – by means of two universal couplings of variable length, attached to the rear extension of the upright. The design works in such a way that a racing car can be converted from the hitherto usual wishbone suspension to the De-Dion system in only a few hours.

156

There are three petrol inlets on the Ferrari 312 T. They will only open if the funnel is placed on top, with its special connector, or if the spring-loaded petrol cap is manually depressed. Whenever petrol is being poured in, a second cap has to be opened to allow the air to escape (his fingers are pressing the cap down in the photo on the right). The cap automatically forms an airtight seal the moment the funnel is lifted off it. The quantity of petrol tanked depends on how much is needed: for test drives the tanks are half-filled, for qualifying laps the quantity will only be enough for a few laps, prior to the start of an actual race up to 230 litres are put in.

158

about six-tenths of a second. Before setting out on the warpath you tank up with only enough petrol for a few laps and you put on a new set of tyres. (In the chapter on tyres we saw that as they no longer manufacture the super-soft special tyres that they used to, we can only put on normal tyres made of 'race compound' rubber.) Then we have to give them the first-warm-up treatment until they attain the 'super grip' characteristics I described in an earlier chapter : this comes a few laps after we begin to run in the tyres, it lasts for only a few laps and then decreases.

When everything is set up – car, timing and tyres – you ought to be able to set off, but there is still a traffic problem : you can only drive really fast laps if nobody gets in your way. This may be because there happens not to be many drivers out on the circuit, or because the slower driver out there proves 'co-operative'. (In this case 'slower' does not reflect in any way on his ability – he may be trying out new adjustments or driving in his tyres or brakes, which means he will be taking the circuit at a moderate speed). Most real top-notch drivers are co-operative when it comes to this. But unfortunately there are also men like Andretti, Stommelen and the late Graham Hill who either do not look in their rear-view mirror enough or are just too stubborn to get out of the way. If you come up behind a driver like this it means that you will have lost that lap and you have got to start it all over again.

My confidence in the co-operative drivers is so extensive that I am able to drive flat out towards many of them – of course you can easily identify them from the rear – because I can be quite sure that the driver will pull over and let me through. If the other man is also doing qualifying laps for the pole position there is of course no way for me to come up on him so fast from behind, because the speed differences would be far too slight – so it will always be a driver who has nothing to lose if he briefly sidesteps or taps his brake pedal to let me pass. This is why I just cannot understand the attitude of the unco-operative drivers – they just senselessly complicate things in our profession.

Let us now have a look at an average circuit that will lap in under two minutes. I have first had my car set up (petrol, tyres) and I am already sitting in it waiting for a good traffic situation : then I drive off. I work things out so that after one or two laps I have got the tyres up to the best temperature. I pay no attention at all to sparing the car, for instance I will allow it to drift over the curbs sometimes – and I would never do that in an actual race. I am driving under extraordinary stress and really giving it everything I have got. (That's why you can imagine how bitter it is to find an unco-operative driver suddenly planting himself in front of you.) If everything really goes off well I often do not even need to get the signal from the pits, because I will know it for myself : that was the best time, or at least that was your own personal best time. And often you get the feeling too that it would be pointless to have another go at it because there would be no way to take it any faster. Of course it will often happen, if several drivers have all got their cars up to the same superb standard, that they will chase each other right up to the very end of the practice period : one man will squeeze another tenth of a second off his time, and by way of reaction from the others' times as well. I remember Brands Hatch in 1974 particularly vividly in this respect : on one day Ronnie and I each had three goes at it, each time we each beat the other's best time. Finally we both had exactly the same time – but I got the pole position, because I had attained mine ten minutes before Ronnie got his.

The reason I get the pole position relatively frequently is surely because I really put my back into the job, both in the preparations beforehand and in the actual battle for the vital lap times.

SLIPSTREAMING

You may have noticed that I have not talked about slipstreaming. On today's race tracks it is of diminishing importance for the practice laps (by which I am referring to 'towing' one another, and not the method of overtaking from out of another car's slipstream during an actual race).

But there are Grand Prix tracks where slipstreaming may work, among them Zeltweg and Paul Ricard. The straights on other top-speed tracks like Silverstone are too short. In earlier years Monza was a typical slipstreaming track, but the chicane there has put an end to that.

What happens is this : the suction created by the front car allows the rear one to drive equally fast but with less engine effort. It works only on the straight and it has side-effects : as the slipstream is no longer smooth, your head is badly knocked about. A loud sound of wind beating is a sure sign that you are hitting the slipstream of the man in front. The water temperature of the rear car rapidly climbs by 5 or 10 degrees C., firstly because the turbulent air is a less effective coolant and secondly because it has been pre-heated by the car in front. So you will not be able to stay in somebody's slipstream for long, with most engines. A further side-effect is that your steering goes 'light', because there is not so much down pressure on your car; this would make your car less manoeuverable on bends.

To get the best out of slipstreaming during the practice laps, two drivers

Slipstreaming: the driver behind knows by the turbulence that he has hit the slipstream of the man in front.

Paul Ricard is one of the few tracks where slipstreaming tactics will in theory help you during the practice laps. During the race slipstreaming groups will always form, but I keep well out of them when I am driving there. The photo shows the starting and finishing straight – in comparison to the two thousand yard long Mistral straight in the opposite direction this one is quite short.

162

would have to get together and really work out a mutual programme; but in practice it never happens (not now, anyway) because nobody wants to haul another man round the track.

But theoretically, it would work out like this : you would only be able to overtake each other in such a way that you get the overtaking business over before you reach the braking zone – because if you force your partner to brake then you have lost all the benefits. The faster man drives ahead on the bend, the rear car sucks into the slipstream, overtakes him on the straight, both take the braking zone strictly according to the book and then the bend as well, then the other car sucks into the slipstream of the front man again, overtakes him from the slipstream and so on. But as said, all the big slipstream antics staged today are wholly unrewarding.

The Race

Now we have reached the race itself. In what follows you will not hear much about emotions, and I think this is quite right too. The movie scenes of racing drivers going off to the start with thumping hearts, meaningful stares into the eyes of their beloved, twitching facial muscles and the like – there just is not any of that to be seen, at least not amongst the men who are really fast. In the interview right at the beginning of this book I talked about 'throwing a switch' in my brain, from human being to racing driver; we really do have a switch like that – we can reduce the art of racing to its basic technological aspects.

You could also put it another way : it is the ability to concentrate entirely on what matters – and emotions just do not have any place on the race track. That is why it is particularly unpleasant as a racing driver to be distracted in any way from your attempt at concentrating. We never have asked for much, we have learned to live with the rough and tumble of it all. As far as I myself am concerned, all I need are the very last few minutes before the race to collect my thoughts, to programme what I am going to do, to throw that switch and concentrate on the job in hand for the next two hours. And if people will not allow me these few moments – when I am already sitting in my car ! – then I do tend to snap at them. There was an absolutely ridiculous scene just before the start at Monaco in 1974 – when I was already edgy enough as we had just had the whole circus with the swap-over of starting places between Regazzoni and me : I was already sitting in my car, trying to put everything around me out of my mind, when a gaggle of Johnny Walker types in top hats waddled up, posed in front of the TV cameras, rabbitted on about something and roared with laughter – and put their hands on my Ferrari. That is when I blew up and brought my fist down on the fingers of one of them. To fly off the handle like that – in other words, to let your emotions get the better of you – is however one of the rare exceptions.

On the pages that follow I will describe a race in the sober atmosphere that genuinely does exist from the driver's vantage point, even if it may not reflect the kind of atmosphere that there is in the pits : because the driver will only be on top of his job if he regards a race as a sequence of situations and combinations of different and changeable factors. The more he has gone over the different possible situations in his mind's eye beforehand, the better he will react when the time comes. And while driving never really deteriorates into a routine (it takes far too much 'punch' for that) there are movements and reactions that you do make virtually automatically. And there can be no room for emotions at all.

This takes us to the point. A sequence of situations and combinations of different and changeable technical factors. The rough and tumble, the hurly-burly outside we have already put out of our minds. Everything now has its place. So we will begin at the beginning.

THE START

We have already mentioned several times the importance of the start. It is not of equal importance everywhere: in Monaco, it may decide the race, at Paul Ricard, with its fine overtaking stretches, rarely ever. Whatever the track, however, you will always do your utmost to get away fast.

Once again a whole host of factors comes into play: your position on the starting grid, the kind of grid, the condition of the road surface (wet or dry), your ratio in first gear, the weather conditions along the track.

Let us just isolate the actual moment of moving off. The art of controlled wheel-spin is the alpha and omega of the start, because it would be impossible to start fast enough using the clutch – letting it slip. You could not even let it slip for just a few yards, because the enormous heat developed would ruin it completely and at once. So you have to let in the clutch with a bang causing the rear wheels to begin spinning immediately: You increase engine revs until a specific rpm is reached – and we will discuss that shortly – you let the clutch in

Wheelspin. '. . . the black marks on the road surface should only be about four inches long, and then fade into a light grey.' Jean-Pierre Jarier (right) at Interlagos, evidently not sticking too closely to the 'instructions'!

with a bang and then you accelerate a bit more.

With a Formula I engine developing some 500 horsepower, it is obvious that you cannot just put your foot down and drive off. Your wheels would begin spinning, but they would slip far too much : you would throw up a lot of smoke and leave long black tyre marks, but you would not have made a good (fast) start.

If I have fitted a relatively short bottom gear, I will go up to 8,000 rpm, if it is a long one then I will go up to 9,000 before letting the clutch in. (In South Africa, where you have less usable horsepower because of the heat, you have to take the Ferrari engine up to 10,000 rpm.) Because of the extra gas used letting the clutch in, there is some wheelspin so I at once decelerate enough to cut the spin slightly and then I allow it to increase again, but this time by engine power alone as the clutch is now securely engaged. The wheelspin at the back will now be about 20 per cent, but quite apart from such theoretical values you yourself will feel accurately what wheelspin gives you the right thrust : you can even determine this externally, because if the wheelspin is ideal (i.e., the thrust is ideal) you will not leave long black marks on the road surface – they should only be about four inches long (i.e., for the very first wheelspin phase) and then fade into a light grey.

So this is what happens at the actual moment of 'take-off'. To understand a very important aspect of the start we first have to look at a special characteristic that is peculiar to thoroughbred racing cars. If the car is at a standstill, in first gear with its engine running the clutch develops so much heat that the free play between the clutch plates is lost (because of thermal expansion). So the car slowly begins to move off, even though the driver does not want it to – the reader will probably have noticed that at some starts and have taken it for a driver's 'over-eagerness'. If the dropping of the starting flag is delayed for any reason by more than about ten seconds, the whole thing can turn very nasty. Your car begins to roll forwards, you have got no hand brake, so you either have to tap the footbrake briefly or hope that the flag drops in the next tenth of a second and you do not get a penalty for a false start. De-selecting the gear is no solution, either, because the clutch is so hot that you cannot even do that. So you are in a real vicious circle and the only way out of it is to foul the start up deliberately and then keep hoping your clutch has some semblance of usability left in it for the rest of the race – and you will find that out soon enough in the first laps.

If we know all these things, then the starting sequence begins to make more sense. Let us look at the items one at a time. I have warmed up my engine, everything has been checked for one last time, I am sitting in my car and I have been finally buckled in. They send us out for a warm-up lap. Something like hysteria breaks out in the pits, although of course all the preparations have long been taken care of; but for a short time everybody transfers bag and baggage from the pits to the pre-start position : that means taking a complete set of spare tyres, compressed air bottle with auto-spanner for the wheel bolts, car jack and all manner of tools so as to be able to make minor repairs. The equipment is all carried to the start line on a little handtruck. As soon as I get back there after warming-up tyres and brake linings, a routine test and check programme is carried out, concentrating mainly on the tyre pressures. More than once we have found a loss of air after the warm-up lap : in a case like that we change the tyre (inside fifteen seconds!) This of course puts our chances of making an optimum get-away at rock bottom : while this new tyre will have been just as carefully 'run in' as the others during these practice laps, it will now be stone cold which means that it does not have the same grip as the others to start with. In a case like this you have to drive very prudently at first.

If the weather looks changeable, you really end up in the tyre-transport business. Because then you also have to take rain tyres to the pre-start line with you. Usually they then wait until it is either really raining or it has cleared up and then they let you drive a couple of laps or so to find out a bit about the new track conditions.

After the last routine checks the tyres are carefully cleaned of any little pebbles or grit. Three minutes before the off all helpers have to clear the track with the exception of one mechanic per car. He plugs in the auxiliary starter battery, two minutes before the start. A last quick glance over the instruments. If the water heats up too much now there is real trouble, because then it may boil over before we start moving : all Formula cars are cooled only by the slip-stream through the radiators, they have no fans.

We are called on to move forwards to our allotted positions on the starting grid. The one-minute board goes up. I select first gear and drive forward to my position. There I go back into neutral immediately, for the reasons already discussed. When the last car is in position and everybody has calmed down, the thirty-second board goes up.

After that the Ten Second board. It does not mean that the start will be in ten seconds' time, but that *within* the next ten seconds the starting flag will drop. You at once select first gear (and like that you cannot wait longer than ten seconds anyway because of the clutch heat) and rev up to the right rpm – in my case 8,000, 9,000 or 10,000 revs. A driver like Regazzoni is not so keen on constant revs, he keeps revving up and down and hopes that when the flag drops he will just be up high enough. You stare at the starting official, hypnotized by every twitch he makes.

I myself will have gone over to the starting official an hour beforehand to say Hello to him and ask him about his method – whether he is going to take it particularly fast, whether he will lower the flag without any hesitation or whether he will make a brief introductory move. If you ask him politely enough he will give a friendly answer and you can interpret it as you wish.

The pack of two dozen Formula I cars is of course just about the most nervous rabble you can imagine (by which I mean the cars and not their drivers), one tremble from one of them and suddenly half the field is moving off without the starting official having batted an eyelash. In a case like that he will drop the flag as fast as he can, because to have to start all over again creates enormous technical problems. If you are the only one to make an obvious premature start the worst that can happen to you is a time penalty – although it can sometimes be quite steep (as much as one minute).

Do the home drivers get a preferential start compared with those 'playing away'? We cannot generalize, but they probably do. The Argentina Grand Prix starts when Reutemann's foot hits the gas pedal.

Of course it is much easier to jump the gun if you're well to the rear of the grid, because then you are not so much under their eagle eyes as the drivers in the first line. Another thing also helps the 'backbenchers': they benefit from certain delayed action effects, so that even if they make only a middling kind of get away they do not drop back several places, while for the pole position driver to make a mistake may easily mean that by the time he has collected himself again a few seconds later he has dropped back to sixth or seventh.

For the sake of completeness, we ought also to mention the starting procedure on a wet track. I myself use second gear, as I find I can control the wheelspin better like that. I will then reach 9,000 revs before letting in the clutch.

The most unpleasant get-away is that at Monte Carlo, where you have a right hand bend just a hundred yards after the starting line; so the inner position is of prime importance here. Only one car will make it – and that means that the outside car will get left behind. If you are not out in front, you have got to use virtually brute force to wriggle through. To take it on the outside is quite hopeless because then you are ploughing through all the filth lying next to the ideal line and at that radius you have to decelerate so much that a whole pack of drivers will thereafter go accelerating past you. You just have to force yourself onto the inside. The pole position man can of course choose what starting position he wants. He will almost always choose that inner position and will ensure logically enough that the position is more or less clean, too. As the inner position is often just next to the ideal line I will drive – assuming that I have won the pole position already – as often as possible over my starting position during the last practice laps, so as to sweep it clean . . . because there is nothing that sweeps cleaner than a Formula I car driving flat out.

If I cast my mind back to the best start in my whole career, then it was the one with the most extraordinary other features too. It was the 1973 Grand Prix at Silverstone, I was driving a BRM and was next to Regazzoni in the fourth row of the grid. When the flag dropped I drove altogether a distance of twelve inches. A half-shaft had broken. Jackie Oliver shunted lightly into my rear, but that was all. I was very fed up as they pushed me back to the pits. But a few minutes later it was obvious to me that my guardian angel must have sawn through the half-shaft : at Woodcote Jody Scheckter went into a spin, crashed into the pit wall and started a mass pile-up involving Hailwood, Beltoise, Mass, Pace, Williamson, de Adamich, Follmer and Hill. The organizers had the whole

Remarkable things happen at the start on the inclined track at Brands Hatch. The Shadow at the left of the photograph has started with too much wheel spin. Because the rear wheels are spinning, they cannot hold the car against lateral forces with the result that the car's rear is swinging over, down the incline. Other cars on the inner lane are also seen to be fighting with the problem.

mess cleared out of the way – and that meant cutting de Adamich free from the wreckage of his Brabham – and during the delay I got hold of the wreck of my team colleague Beltoise's car and put one of his half-shafts in my car. When the race was re-started an hour and a half later I was still in the fourth row but there was a gap in the grid in front of me because Scheckter had dropped out. I got away like greased lightning, passed Stewart and Cevert and when the first bend came I was right on the tail of Ronnie Peterson, who was out in front. He hit the brakes unusually early which irritated me – I thought he must have had some reason like an oil smear on the track – so I did not overtake him though in fact I could have done. No matter : it was a super start, because at one fell swoop I had overtaken Cevert, Reutemann, Stewart, Fittipaldi, Hulme and Revson. When all was said and done it did not give me the race, however, because my left front tyre began to play up; but the memory of that fine start still gives me a little glow of pleasure.

The anti-climax to Silverstone in 1973 was Nürburgring in 1974. To help understand the debâcle there, I must flashback to the previous Grand Prix and that was at Brands Hatch : I had the pole position there next to Peterson, which put me a bit uphill from him, so I did not think I had much chance against Ronnie but I still managed a superb start. The 'magic rev number' at Brands Hatch was to hit precisely 8,000 rpm when you let the clutch in. Since these 8,000 rpm turned out to be perfect for a start under difficult conditions like those at Brands Hatch I decided to stick with them at the Nürburgring. Again I had got the pole position, this time I was next to Regazzoni who was my biggest rival for the world championship. I knew him well and figured that I could demoralize him so much by a flying start and two flat-out laps that the race would have to go my way. My first mistake was that I had not taken into account that at Nürburgring I had taken 30 litres more petrol on board than two weeks before at Brands Hatch. That meant that the 8,000 rpm just were not enough, I lost revs badly and got away so miserably that all of a sudden I was only lying third. At that moment I should have been smart enough to ditch my battle plan of flying out ahead of him; but I was not. I grit my teeth and tried to pull it off by brute force. I at once tried to out brake Jody Scheckter, so as not to lose contact with Regazzoni. Normally that would have worked okay, but that was when when I made mistake Number Two: I had forgotten all about my right front tyre. What had happened was this : at the pre-start position we had had to change a tyre, because on the drive over from the drivers' quarters to the pits it had lost pressure. Normally you do not drive that stretch on the actual race tyres, but with other tyres so as not to run any risks on this dirty stretch. The proper tyres are then only fitted in the pits. But as we were all working under pressure that day we had made an exception and changed the tyres round at the drivers' quarters. Normally that would not have mattered, as a complete Nürburgring lap of thirteen miles as an introductory lap still lay ahead which would easily have sufficed to drive in the new tyres. But unfortunately it began to rain slightly during this introductory lap so I had to drive the whole lap very cautiously. The new tyre was not properly warmed up in consequence, so it had not yet attained maximum grip. I forgot clean about it, but was reminded of it very brutally when I trod on the brake pedal at my braking-point before the north hairpin, the second bend after the start. The car swung so sharply that I collided with Scheckter and ended up in the safety fence. The lesson : you cannot go off into real battle if your tyres have not been equally run in.

RACING ROUTINE

The more or less mechanical actions in driving a car are part of the racing routine, as I already described, as are the observation of the instruments and the signals from the pits.

The attention I pay to the instruments varies. If I am just battling it out with an opponent, I will try and let the instruments distract me as little as possible. But if I have got time and my opponents well in hand then all my attention is devoted to the instruments alone – not that there is a great deal I can do if they do deviate from normal readings.

My primary attention goes to the rev counter, before each time I come up to the rev limit. With experience you can estimate your engine revs pretty

'First' to get away in the rain at Zolder, 1975. (The final victor, Hunt, is lying third here, behind Scheckter.)

FORMULA I DRIVERS: THE FACE OF A PROFESSION.

Mario Andretti

Vittorio Brambilla ▲

Patrick Depailler ▼

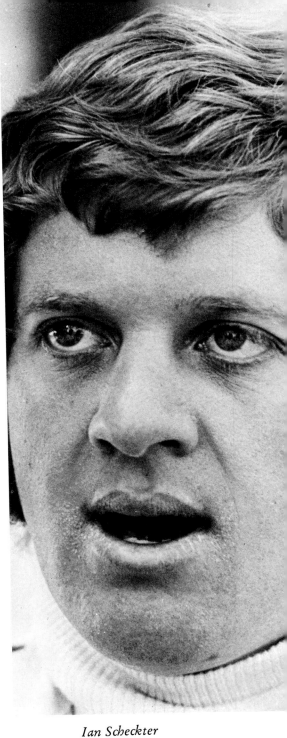

Ian Scheckter

Emerson Fittipaldi

Bob Evans ▲   *James Hunt* ▶

Ronnie Peterson ▼

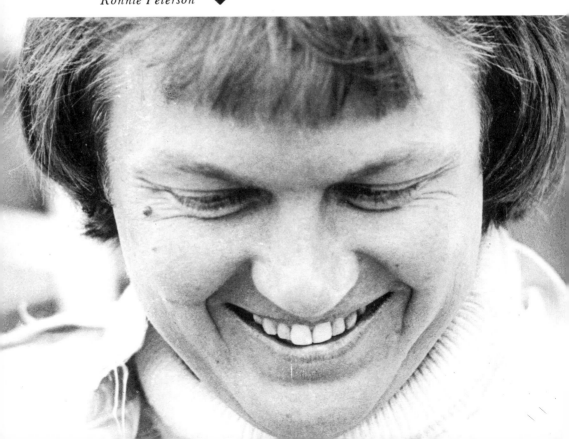

Jacky Ickx

Jean-Pierre Jarier

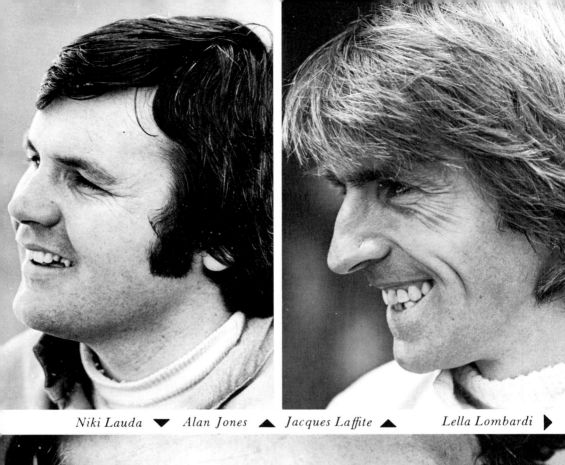

Niki Lauda ▼ Alan Jones ▲ Jacques Laffite ▲ Lella Lombardi ▶

Jochen Maas   *Gunnar Nilsson*

Clay Regazzoni

Jody Scheckter

Carlos Reutemann   *Hans-Joachim Stuck* ▶

Rolf Stommelen

John Watson ▶

closely from its note; I myself start looking at around 12,000 rpm and my eyes stay glued to it for the remaining 300 up to my limit.

I check the rest of the instruments as and when the pressure I am under allows me to. If possible once each lap, or perhaps only once every other lap; if the worst comes to the worst it might be ten laps between checks . . . provided everything is still running okay and my engine sounds sweet, everything has a good feel and the maximum revs are reached according to programme.

What can I actually do if any instrument tells me that something's wrong? The point is this: there is not a lot you can do, the instruments have far more importance during the practice laps than during a race, because during the practice laps you are still a free man and you can adjust something on the car or undertake repairs. To stop at the pits is virtually a thing of the past nowadays (except for a tyre change). Even a simple topping up the water level would mean losing the race: open up the engine cover, open the cap, water goes in, boils over and so on . . . it is almost pointless.

One thing you can act on is the water temperature: if it climbs too high, then you cut back on the revs. If the temperature then stays constant, you have a good chance that it is just something minor, perhaps a bit of paper obstructing a radiator. Of course it might be an oil cooler that is obstructed like this, but here too lower revs will bring the required reaction. If the only warning lamp on the panel lights up, then it is the oil pressure: and then there is almost never anything you can do about it. But if this happens just before the finish (as at Monaco in 1975 to me) then you can just about save yourself over that distance by taking the bends relatively slowly.

But if there is not much that you can do about instruments except hope they all stay on your side, signals from the pits really do demand your attention. This display each lap is really vital to me. If the mechanics forget to hold out the sign board that is one of the very few things that really irritates me so much that I lose my temper. Of course if I am the meat in the sandwich, with one opponent ahead of me and another behind, the board is not all that important to me – I can see with my own eyes how things are, whether there is any change

Out comes the umbrella: 1975 was the rainy season for races.
Start at Zandvoort: Lauda, Scheckter, Hunt, Regazzoni, Fittipaldi.
Carlos Reutemann, Brabham.
Brands Hatch 1976, Hunt and Lauda.
Emerson Fittipaldi, McLaren.

or not. But if I am not right on their heels I have to be kept right up to date. On the board I can see under LAUDA the precise lead of the man in front and my lead over the man following me marked in seconds + or − (to the nearest tenth of a second). For the last twenty laps a second board is also displayed: so-and-so many laps still to go. Normally you can clearly recognize your own boards, you only have problems on tracks where the pits are on the far side of a bend (like at Silverstone).

Why is such precise information so vital to me? Because you should only drive as fast as is necessary to win. If I am lying first and they show me + 10 and I still have ten laps to go, then I will drop back about one second per lap . . . and that is what the others also do if they are in front, particularly the really cool and intelligent drivers like Fittipaldi. What looks like the 'drama' of the finish is often nothing more than the leader's deliberating slackening off, to spare his own car.

How far your own pit will manipulate the figures to stimulate you, I cannot judge from my own experience. I think it only happens rarely, because they assume I am sensible enough to do the proper thing. But I once saw one thing that annoyed me: I was leading Regazzoni, my pit showed me + 30; but I could also see the other board that they were going to show Regazzoni and that one read − 20. I was annoyed, because I want to be able to rely one hundred per cent on what my pit tells me.

FIGHTING FOR POSITION AND TACTICS

An incidental sentence casually written in the last section says virtually all there is to say about 'tactics' nowadays: you should only drive as fast as is necessary to win. And if you are not in the winning position, then your tactics are just as simple: drive as fast as you can. 'Tactical devices' and 'tactical secrets' are just things dreamed up by the journalists . . . unless you call it tactics to make as fast a getaway as possible, to pull ahead of your opponents as fast as possible and then to drive as sparingly as possible and to go out there and win.

Of course if an individual driver has no tactics − because he cannot have any − then this is even more true for a team: there is no such thing as team tactics. At most there may be something of a priority inside one of those teams with an obviously superior driver like for instance McLaren's in the 1975 season with Fittipaldi and Tyrrell's with Scheckter − then you might find that at the finish the number 2 man will let the number 1 stay in front if it will help number 1 towards the World Championship. But when the teams had drivers

of equal ability – Regazzoni & myself, Pace & Reutemann, Ickx & Peterson – there were no such courtesies. For me Regazzoni is a rival like the rest and I fight him like any other . . . nor do I expect any courtesy from him once we are out on the track. That can only change if one of us stands a chance of becoming world champion and the other does not have even a theoretical chance, as in 1974 for example in the very last race at Watkins Glen – then of course I would have helped Clay there if I could have. So brainwork during the actual race will never be of as much use to you as before it begins, on the adjustment and of the car and mental preparation for certain events. My victory in the Grand Prix in Sweden in 1975 was certainly mainly due to my having chosen the harder tyre compound while all my opponents were driving the normal compound. Naturally it looked like 'tactics' on my part during the race : there I was driving slower at the start, and there I am in the lead when it finishes : people might imagine I deliberately 'held back' at the beginning, but this was nonsense, I drove flat out the whole time, and had the greatest difficulty in keeping up at all to start with but then when the desired tyre effect came on I just pulled ahead. But the action that mattered was what I had done beforehand; once the race began there was nothing I could do but drive flat out.

OVERTAKING

Overtaking is less and less of the pleasure that it used to be. Given the almost identical cars that we now have, to overtake even a slower driver is downright impossible from the purely theoretical point of view. Take Monaco, an extreme case : braking point and entry into the bends each follow in such close succession that you never get the time to build up enough excess speed. That means that any overtaking in Monaco nowadays is attributable either to a car defect or a driving error by the man in front (or his good will). If you are the attacker there is nothing else you can do than loom as large as you can in the other man's rear view mirror, keep up the pressure on him and hope he makes a slip. That is why you can never let up, never let him out of striking distance, because when he makes that slip you have got to be right in there to exploit it without a moment's hesitation.

These boards inform me that I have a 1.2 second lead on Regazzoni and that I am 3.3 seconds ahead of Fittipaldi, with four more laps to go. If things are as clear cut as in this case, they will often dispense with adding my name to the board. Normally the name LAUDA would be added at the foot of the big board.

Fortunately there are other racing tracks where overtaking is still a fine art allowing you to use your best skills.

From the driving seat of the man in front things look like this. If somebody just comes up from behind me and overtakes – just like that – it can mean only one thing : something is wrong with my car. Normally he will only be able to come on slowly, take up station behind me and put on the pressure. Every time I leave a bend I take a look in my mirror to see if he has come any nearer or if he has dropped back. After a time I will know just how his car is behaving, in what respects it is better than mine and where it is inferior. The factor that matters is the speed difference as we leave those bends – that is the foundation of virtually every overtaking manoeuvre. If there are five bends, say, and in three of them I am (only fractionally) slower than him, but equally fast in the other two, then I have a good chance to keep him put. In my 'good' curves I keep the speed up, and in his good curves I just do as good as I can. The real attack can only come at a very few places along the track – frequently only at one : then his car has to nose right forward, until he's only a few inches behind mine, suddenly swing out just before the next bend and try to reach the inner lane on that bend before I can. 'Sealing off' that inner lane – not to be confused with dangerous zigzagging on the straight! – is absolutely legitimate and a perfectly viable means of defence for the person under attack, so the attacker must always take this possibility into account.

But from the driving seat of the pursuer it looks like this : I must above all try and irritate the man in front. For lap after lap I have been studying him, I know the strengths and weaknesses of his car, know whether it is under- or over-steering, know what his top speed is. From these factors a particular point along the track will crystallize for me – but that does not mean that I will not feint attacks at other points as well. I must keep bobbing up at different points in his rear mirror, sometimes on the left, sometimes on the right, then left, then three times on his right and left again and then next time right out of his field of mirror view : I have got to give him something to worry about all the time. So I will also make as if to overtake him even though I know that nothing is likely to come of it. Not that I am going to get stuck right in to his rear wheels, not at first anyway. I will try to come right up to him after leaving a bend, get into his slipstream until I am only a few inches behind him and then swing out with my extra speed and head straight for the inner track on the next bend. If

One of the most unpleasant moments in racing: overtaking in a rain race, through the spray of the car in front.

200

I do not clear him absolutely cleanly and we both hit the brakes at just the right moment than I still have no chance, because he will 'seal it off' – but I will still keep on trying the same trick time after time. He only has to hit that brake once at the wrong moment and thus miss his ideal line on to the inner track – and I will be through and on the inside myself.

Overtaking on slow bends is obviously not on (every man is driving the same speed); but it is also out of the question on fast bends, because the slipstream effect does not 'work' there. The air turbulence caused by the lead car reduces the down pressure on the following car so much that his steering becomes over light; on the straight this is unimportant, but on bends it is fatal – the car's entire aerodynamics are wrong and it does not respond properly to the controls at all. So you almost always begin your overtaking move as you leave the bend, you execute it on the straight and you complete it by the time you hit the braking point. Distracting the driver in his selection of the right braking moment is one of the pursuer's main weapons. Let me describe my two finest duels from the 1975 season by way of examples :

Anderstop. The sequence is Reutemann – Pace – Lauda. To get at Reutemann I've first got to cross swords with Pace, but this turns out to be a far more laborious process than expected. First I study him : we both accelerate equally well out of the bends, the braking also seems the same to me, but his final velocity on the straights is a bit higher than mine. So for the time being I have no chance, I can only crowd in on his rear mirror and get on his nerves. For about 20 laps virtually nothing changes, I am driving flat out just to keep that position up, no thought of overtaking him. At last Pace makes a mistake : he brakes a bit late, misses his ideal line and he's over in the dirt, has to lift his accelerator foot briefly and slithers sideways to the outside track (on a left hand bend). Of course I drive on to the inside and put my foot down. He is floundering about on the outside – another yard and he would have been on the grass, but regains control of his car and hits the gas pedal at the same moment as I am neck and neck with him. We come out of that bend at the same moment as each other, and go bombing into a right hand bend – and now of course he has the edge on me because he is on the inside. So I drop back again like a good boy and decide that I can only make use of an error by him on the straight – he cannot allow himself any error on the bend before the straight; and that is why I step up the

The big gamble of the 1975 season: how far should the track have dried out before you swap your rain tyres for slicks? (In this picture: Reutemann, Mass and Pace, all still driving slicks).

pressure on him just there on each lap, I come to within a yard of him each time. He knows as well as I do what the situation would be if he braked too late, went too far to the outside, and had to slacken off : because this slackening would hit him on the straight and I would get past him. And in fact the moment does come – he does brake too late, I can see his rear sliding over. But that man has guts, and one thing he won't do : and that is slacken off just now. He doesn't let go, tries to control the car, fights with the controls, fights and fights – until he is in a spin and shoots off the inside of the track (he is a lucky man, because he misses a track official fenced in by guard rails only by inches).

Now came the overtaking that mattered, Reutemann, to put me in the lead. Here the situation was very different. First, I could not slipstream any closer to him than his rear wheels, and that is no use at all, because even the boldest braking contest is not going to help if you are more than ten inches behind the nose of the other car. But his tyres were getting worse and worse – I could tell that by the way his Brabham was oversteering. So he had to slacken off on the exit from a bend, and I got my nose level with the middle of his car. In this formation we battle down the straight towards the constriction (a particular Anderstorp refinement!) but here I was on the 'right' side and he had to take his foot off the gas – so I was in front.

These two overtaking manoeuvres look totally different but they have one common factor, one of the most important rules in the art of position-warfare : Thou shalt keep thy Opponent under constant pressure, thou shalt not just dawdle along in his wake without a fight just because thou hast no real chance of overtaking there. You will never get such a chance, if you just hang back like a good boy. In the actual case described, Pace would never have made his braking error with all its consequences if I had not crowded in on his rear-view mirror all the time. And if I had not kept up the pressure on Reutemann either, he could have driven slower and spared his tyres, then he would never have begun oversteering, the defect that enabled me to overtake him too.

The fact is that if the equipment is almost identical every top class driver will be equally difficult to overtake. There is no difference at all between them, you cannot say I would prefer this or that, driver, or he was harder or easier than the others to overtake. By top class drivers I think of (in alphabetical order)

A quick get-away after a tyre change: note that some of the mechanics are wearing gloves against the extreme heat transmitted to the wheel nuts from the brake discs.

Fittipaldi, Hunt, Peterson, Reutemann, Scheckter always, and Depailler, Jarier, Regazzoni sometimes.

WHAT ARE THE CHANGES DURING THE RACE?

Cars, drivers and even the track surface can change during a race. Most people realize that the way a car handles depends on how much petrol load is in the tanks. Many designers have tried to achieve a car that is as neutral in this respect as possible. Others have paid less attention to it, so their cars behave differently. With the Ferrari 312 T we find that when its tanks are full it oversteers rather more noticeably, but that this tendency declines as the tanks empty. This is a benign tendency that causes no problems.

That the tyres also change because of excessive wear or high temperatures has been mentioned. But we keep finding new 'mysterious' changes that are something of a surprise. The most recent was during our practice laps for the Grand Prix in Sweden in 1975. The tyres lost their performance without any visible signs why (normally you can tell when a tyre is nearing the end of its life by the particular shape of the rubber granules). We had to rack our brains to find out even that it was the tyres that were causing the oversteering – whatever we did, the oversteering got worse until we put on a new set of tyres and then found the car to be understeering. The probable explanation for this phenomenon was this : at Anderstorp the two U-bends subject the wheels to extremely long lateral pressures, and this must have somehow distorted the tyre carcass and effectively made the tyres softer.

Does the engine change? Well, we know that the engine loses about twenty horsepower of its performance during a race but you hardly notice this loss – the engine behaves at the finish just the same as it did at the start . . . assuming it has not broken down altogether, which hardly ever happens with the Ferrari engine.

Clutch, gears, suspensions and even the brakes (!) have been perfected to such a degree that you will not observe any change in them during the whole race; on the last lap I can still count on having full braking power.

But the track surface can alter very considerably during the race. For instance, when a car loses more oil than average (because minute quantities are always being lost anyway). Lost oil runs first into a car's catch tank but it may slop over on bends. An oil patch on the track can cause chaos.

Normally the track becomes a bit more slippery because of the oil that all the cars lose and the tyre deposits, and this is why successive laps may be

Tools that have to be handled very deftly if no time's to be lost but the job still has to be done properly: air guns.

slower rather than faster (as we might expect because the petrol tanks are getting lighter). In any case this track surface deterioration means that our fastest lap times in the race are never as good as our best times on the practice laps.

In general there is no change in the driver himself during a race, because he ought to be able to put on his best physical and mental performance for about two hours. Of course many drivers have their own peculiarities : they need a certain warming-up period, or they let their opponent get them down and they lose punch in consequence. What makes a race hardest for the driver is if he has taken the lead right from the start, he has improved this lead and now has to make sure he keeps it : it is sensible now to drive a bit slower, you keep close count of the laps that are left and keep a sharp ear tuned for strange sounds – you even think you hear sounds that do not exist. Then the race seems to last weeks. But even then your training should have got you to such a pitch that you can give of your best until the last moment.

You also ought to be able to put up with any minor pain or discomforts for the relatively short time that a Grand Prix race lasts, and not let them affect your driving. Among these are the obligatory blister on the palm of your right hand (caused by the gear changing), and the neck pains at Interlagos caused by the extreme centrifugal forces and the strain of keeping your heavy helmet upright.

Many drivers find they are bothered by sweat running into their eyes and inflaming them (you cannot rub your eyes because of the visor). I think Jaussaud suffered most from this, he used to wear a headband of towelling under his helmet. I have only heard about the problem, as I myself hardly perspire at all.

You should hardly ever be bothered by wind blowing uncomfortably into the helmet, because you should have spotted this during the practice laps and asked for the windscreen to be raised. Normally the windscreen comes up to mid-nose level. This gives you some protection, if you duck, against flying objects (like bits of rubber and pebbles) and birds. If this narrow strip that I have referred to rather over-elegantly as a windscreen has the right dimensions you ought to have no wind problems at all – you notice it, but it does not bother you.

RAIN RACES AND TYRE CHANGES

Racing in the rain has its own rules and is jam-packed with technical nuances where no amount of forethought is going to be the complete answer . . . you are dependent far more on compromises and improvisations than normally.

If it was dry during the practice laps and it is raining on the day of the race, the car's set-up has to be completely changed. The car is made 'softer', so that it 'rolls' more, this gives it better road holding and the driver has more feel for the car's behaviour. Cars that push their nose outwards are particularly poor to handle in the rain, so you will try to set-up an over-steering situation : you will put a lot of wing on in front to increase the down pressure on the front axle, you will strengthen the rear anti-roll bar and weaken the front one. You will make this adjustment instinctively at first and then re-adjust it after a short practice. I find such rain adjustments are right and proper if the car is reacting **very** strongly to the accelerator pedal and if it is a way of helping me out to take corrective action with that pedal.

That our extra wide tyres positively aid the tendency to aquaplane is of course

A race to change tyres on the day before the 1975 Grand Prix at Silverstone: Tyrrell won, Ferrari lost not only this demonstration but also next day when the tyre changes were made in real earnest.

obvious. So you take good care when driving through puddles, and you may even have slots cut additionally into the centre of the tyres to offset this.

If nobody gives any of his opponents any quarter at the start on a normal race day, they certainly do not if it is raining because the battle is much tougher – overtaking is much harder than usual. The start is that much more important.

One of the hardest jobs in Formula I driving is the pioneer work of the first few laps, particularly if it was dry during the practice laps : because now you will have no data to go on, and have to work out every braking and gear-change point all over again – going by instinct alone. By the time you have collected enough data to go by, the whole situation may well have changed again.

You will know the feeling of driving in another car's back spray from your own experience of motorway driving. You have to have nerves to keep right up with the man in front and then risk overtaking. Your visibility problems are caused in racing not only by the spray, but also by your visor steaming up. You can't get at it with your hand, so various people have devised various technical solutions. There are already heated visors that plug into the car's electrical system. But there is still no complete answer, because even heating cannot prevent air turbulence from forcing water up inside the helmet. The worst thing of all is if your visor steams up right at the start, the moment you close it. I often see the man next to me frantically flapping his visor up and down and wiping it clean. Nature has given me a simple system that is in fact highly professional : because of my buck teeth it is an easy matter for me to breath out in a downward direction !

And now the most complex of all possible cases : the race starts wet, then dries out. You will have had to make up your mind about the car's adjustments before the start and now you will have to make do with the car as it is, because the time used for the tyre change is too short to make even the most minor adjustment to the car. But a car that was properly set up for rain conditions is not going to be right for a dry surface – no way. Just how nasty the car's temperament now turns is largely a matter of luck. Not just because of the over soft adjustments, because there are the brakes and the brake-pressure distribution to consider too : a car set up for dry racing will overbrake in the front in rainy conditions, which is quite frightful; and conversely a car set up for rain racing will retard poorly in the dry, because you will have put too much of the braking pressure on the rear axle.

When the ideal line has already dried out and you are already beginning to flounder on your rain tyres, the big moment comes for your pit team. We only have to consider how hard it is to gain fifteen seconds by driving faster; and how easy it is to lose the same fifteen seconds by one single slip during the tyre change, to realize how important this tyre change can be. The pit teams have often practised this routine, the Ferrari crew's record is seventeen seconds for a complete all-round tyre change.

If they are expecting a driver to come in for a tyre change, they have everything ready and waiting: four men with air guns, two men with rapid-duty jacks and a director. First the driver has to get it right: he has to drive up to the pit area just right, because the air guns do not have much room for play (they are connected by high-pressure lines to air bottles), and besides the new tyres are already waiting at the proper positions. Stop, engine off, simultaneously the car is already being jacked up front and rear, and the four air guns are slammed into action. With an air gun the wheel does not turn itself, so it does not need either ground contact or to be held in some other way. The wheels of Formula I cars have only one big central nut, with left-hand or right-hand thread according to which side of the car. The heavy air guns – which are by no means all that easy to handle – can be switched from one motion to the other: this is one of the biggest chances of getting things wrong in a tyre change; another possible mistake is to cross thread the nut when putting it back on – this is relatively easy to do, as the nut is deep down inside the wheel rim (and quite apart from that the brake discs have heated up everything so much that the mechanics have to work with gloves). The jacks can only be let down again if all the nuts have been completely tightened, as otherwise the wheels will not be perfectly aligned. You can only tell if the nuts have been tightened enough from the sound of the air guns as they hammer away: if one of them is out of harmony, then a tyre may come off on the next bend – it happens all too often. The engine can only be restarted once the car has touched down again, as otherwise the rear wheels might begin to spin which would hamper the mechanics. I then get the signal to go from the 'director', who has taken up station ahead of the car throughout the routine. It all sounds very remarkable, it has the ring of planning and organisation, but it can all go very cock-eyed indeed as it did in the Grand Prix at Silverstone in 1975: the badly tightened front wheel resulted in both personnel changes (different mechanic duties) and technical improvements (a better thread).

The only additional adjustment that can be undertaken during the brief period of a tyre change, is to put more or less sticky tape over the brake-ventilation or cooler intakes. Usually it gets marginally warmer when it stops raining, so it makes sense to take off some of the sticky tape.

MY TOUGHEST RACE

This was at the same time my hardest, best and finest race – 1975 in Monaco. There were many combined aspects that overlapped and made this race something unique for me even before the start.

It all began on the evening of the previous race, the tragic Barcelona meeting. Most people were talking of boycotting ordinary street tracks, and Ferrari's were no exception. That same evening Montezemolo phoned me in my hotel room and asked if I would agree to Ferrari's not joining in the start at Monaco. I refused, said I was against any hasty decisions. A little later the Commendatore phoned me in person and wanted my opinion whether to boycott Monaco or not. I told him I thought it should go ahead. That was that on the subject and each man went about his work preparing for the race. The time came for the last checks at Fiorano and the cars to be loaded aboard the transporters. At the factory the Commendatore asked a colleague to remind me : Ferrari has not won at Monaco for twenty years. It was obvious that winning this race was important, emotionally, for everybody at Ferrari's. So even as we departed there was a certain psychological pressure on Regazzoni and myself.

Practice laps : I lapped at 1 minute 27.1 seconds, a fantastic time, it was bound to set me up for the pole position. The practice laps went on another twenty minutes but to be on the safe side I stayed in my car. That's when the news suddenly came that Tom Pryce had done it in 1 minute 26.8. So I had to get out there again. It was what can only be described an 'optimum lap' – I drove flat out and faultlessly. I did not even have to inquire what my time had been, I drove straight back to the drivers' quarters and got out because I knew I could never drive faster than that. In fact they timed it at 1 minute 26.4, Pryce's time was later officially confirmed at 1 minute 27.09. So that gave me a seven-tenths' lead on him in the fastest practice lap – and seven-tenths is an eternity. That piled up even more pressure on me, because now the Italian newspapers were writing that a Ferrari victory at Monaco was now just a matter of form. For them to proclaim 'victory' even before the race is never good from the driver's point of view, and I was not very happy about the situation.

Zolder 1975, Brambilla.
Hunt and Lauda, 1976.
Watson Rocket.
Fire extinguishing.
The pits at Zolder, Fittipaldi.

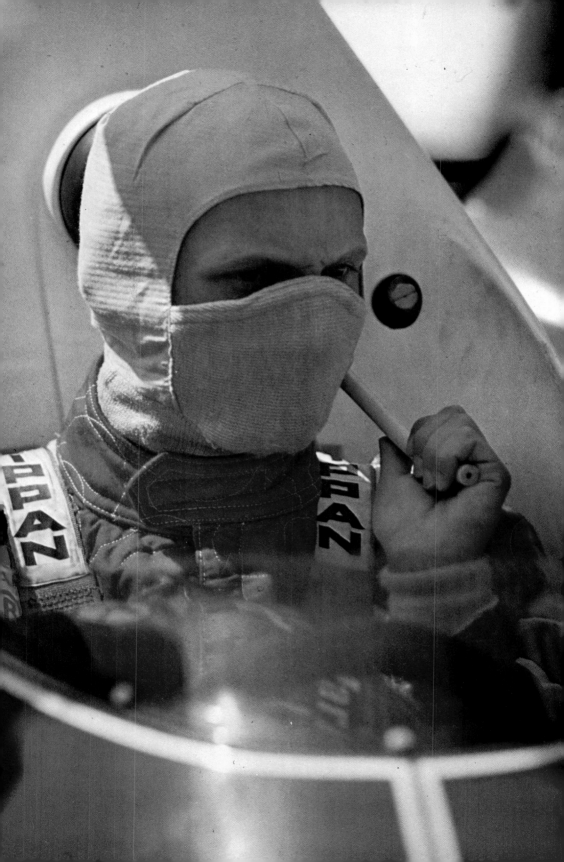

On the morning of the race I glanced out of the window : raining. That meant no more Ferrari supremacy, no talk of seven-tenths per lap, we would have to set-up the cars all over again and each of us would have the same chances. On top of this the burden of having to get the best possible advantage out of that pole position, and then the pressure that bears down on every lead driver, particularly in the rain because he has to work out new braking and gear-change points by instinct alone,while everybody behind him is just waiting for him to make a slip. I think I can say I have never driven as well as on that day. Everything – but everything, went perfectly : not one fault, no uncertainty, it was my day and my race. Neither before nor since have I had so much pleasure in a victory.

MY EASIEST RACE

No doubt about it. I never had it so easy as at Zandvoort in 1974. I made the best practice time without any particular difficulty, Regazzoni lay next to me in the first row of the starting grid. I made a copy book get-away, Regazzoni and the other top men were not quite so well placed, so I had a clear lead right from the start. Then it emerged that there was nobody there able or willing to attack me. But I did not get bored myself, because I could always keep my ears on the engine note and my eyes every second or so on the instruments; otherwise there was not much else to do. I came away with a relaxed victory, and did not even feel tired afterwards.

MY MOST DANGEROUS SITUATION

Again no doubt about it : it was 1976, on the Nürburgring . . . but as I said earlier there is not much I can say about it because I have no memory of it, absolutely no memory at all. I only know the situations I had to survive afterwards, and they were dramatic enough : in the hospital. There were big crises involving both my lungs and my blood. In some kind of way I knew what was happening : I had no willpower at first, I was weary, apathetic – you just want to glide away and you have no urge at all to do anything against dying. While I was drifting around in this fog of semi-consciousness I suddenly thought I heard the name Fittipaldi. Fitt's doctor had come to the hospital to see if there was any way he could help with his specialized knowledge. Suddenly my brain had something to fasten on to, I began to realize bit by bit just why he was here, and what was his name again? what he wanted and so on. That started my brain working again and it was my first step towards wanting to survive. Then Marlene came, and luckily they let her in at once. She sat down there and began talking, and that again gave my brain something to do. Of course I could not speak and could not see, my hearing was my only lifeline to the real world. By next day my brain was working well enough again for me to be able to take something like a formal decision to try to survive. I was aware of the increasing congestion of my lungs and knew that the doctors needed my help. That gave me a target to go for, and it kept me active. That is why people praised my desire to live afterwards. Provided I can think, I can fight.

Aside from this extremely bad accident, my nastiest moment was at the Nürburgring in 1973 when I was driving for BRM. I had driven the fifth best practice lap and in those days (particularly in a BRM) that was very good; in the race too I was also lying well to the fore, in fourth place after the first lap. At the Bergwerk – a second-gear right hand bend – I noticed the car was understeering badly. At first I thought I had gone over a patch of oil. Right after that you hit fifth gear again quite soon, and coming into a fast left-right combination I suddenly lost control over the car (we found out later that something had snapped on the rear wheel suspension). I went into zigzags – I was able to deal with the first few, then the car touched a curb on the right and it was promptly catapulted over to the left of the track. The left front wheel slammed into a sloping rock, sending such a shock up the steering column that I broke

Lauda's crashed Ferrari burning on the track at Nürburgring.

my right wrist. That was the first thought that hit me: my hand's hurting. Then I was tobogganing along this slope and all I could think of was: don't get turned over or you will end up in a situation similar to the one that killed Roger Williamson a few weeks ago. Then there is a hiatus in my recollections, the next thing after that I know is I am slithering towards a track official's hut. Then another gap, but somehow I got past that box and ended up at a standstill eighty yards further on. Some time later they measured my toboggan-run – it was nearly 400 yards long. It would only have taken the slightest thing to have tipped the car right over, and then it would have been no laughing matter.

MY DECISION IN JAPAN (October 1976)

Meantime, I have lost the world championship. I would like to add my own comment to this, as the outcome ultimately hinged on just one race.

The Grand Prix track in Japan was completely new territory to me. I would be inclined to describe it as fast but not extremely difficult; I would even admit that it was a track particularly suited to the Ferrari. The practice laps were also encouraging. The new wheel suspension proved its worth and while I often lay five or six tenths of a second behind the pole position in the most recent races, this time I managed to get into the second starting row, about three-tenths behind the driver with the fastest lap, Mario Andretti.

On the day of the race it had been raining ever since early morning. On the Sunday morning practice I soon realized that under such conditions you just could not drive. The track surface is as worn out as the average German auto-bahn, at some places the water was several inches deep and there was absolutely no tyre adhesion at all. You could not get rid of the constant danger of aqua-planing out of control. After five laps I drove back to the pits and climbed out. That is when an interminable debate began. All the drivers agreed with me except for the March trio – Hans Stuck, Ronnie Peterson and Vittorio Brambilla – and the late Tom Pryce. So in the circumstances we did not make the start. I repeat: we were all in agreement.

The start had been scheduled originally for 1 p.m. About three o'clock that afternoon the race director surprised us all with an alarm call: starting flag in half an hour or it will get too dark before the race is over. It was barely credible: it was now raining heavier than ever, and I asked the people responsible if they could imagine what would happen. They reassured me that fire-engines had pumped away the puddles on the track. Shaking my head I climbed into the car and went out for a warm-up. On the first warm-up lap I had the first fright:

there was John Watson spinning out of control just next to me, by a miracle he did not ram me but tobogganed out onto the grass. And all that was in second gear, with no pressure on us.

I did not make a bad getaway at all, but on the very first bend, lying third, I realized that this was no race for me. After two laps I quit.

Let me make one thing quite clear : my decision had nothing whatever to do with my Nürburgring accident. I am back driving at the limit, my own personal maximum limit, even after that. But Japan topped that limit just as if it had been snowing or if Fuji had erupted. Then there would have been no race either. If others choose to drive, they have every right to do so; but then I must make it plain that when we took our vote they were all – apart from a handful – against it.

I am never going to let any more race managers blackmail me. There must not be any more Barcelonas ! I have got to say that I regard the men who allowed the race in Japan to proceed as lunatics. I afterwards met with the complete approval of my sponsors and of Ferrari's, as I had hoped.

Of course now it is all a matter of history, I was the loser. By a miracle, there was no pile-up, James Hunt is world champion and people have talked themselves blue in the face postulating on my own chances, had I stayed in. But what would the people have said if Hunt had had worse tyre trouble, or if his wheelchange had not gone like clockwork ? I can just imagine how they would all be cooing : Now Lauda, he had brains – he saw all that coming. But that is not how things went : I had to make up my mind when the race was only one and a half laps old and it was blue murder to be out racing on that track. That was before the track began to dry out, before Hunt hit tyre problems. Of course people argue that I used to be a good rain race driver and I won them too, like Oulton Park. But today I look at things differently from a few years ago. And secondly I am as willing now as I ever was to drive in the rain. But there is rain and *rain* : there are differences. And you have to make do with the factors you have got – the cars and the tyres that we race with today.

MY FAVOURITE RACE TRACK

I include this section only because I am always being asked about my 'favourite race' or my 'favourite track'. But I do not have a favourite track, and I do not want to begin thinking in terms of whether I like a particular track or not. I approach every race in the same frame of mind and your own feelings really must not come into it. If any one track seems to give me more problems than the others, then I just have to try and get over them during the training. There was only ever one track that I might mention as not really being my cup of tea : that was Crystal Palace. I did not like driving there at all and I was glad to see the end of it. There were bends there that at that time I just could not manage properly. I was there twice, twice I failed the qualifying rounds and ended up with my car going into a wall. If it had stayed open Crystal Palace might have become something of an Angst-track for me. But that is really the only exception, as otherwise I have no bogey or favourite tracks.

Fitness

At school I was never more than average at gymnastics or sports, I was neither conspicuously bad nor good at them. In fact I was a bit of a physical weakling and I noticed it when I came to drive the Porsche 908 – my arms were not strong enough and I used to get tired very early on. So I made a concerted attack on this weakness, by going to the Fitness Centre in Vienna's Kreuzgasse and going in for bodybuilding work there with dumb-bells and everything else they had. I gained twenty pounds in weight – which brought me up to my present ideal weight of 141 pounds (I am 5 feet 9 inches tall). Sometimes I may put on weight during the season to around 150 pounds, and I have to lose them again during the winter training season.

What matters most for my physical well-being is sleep : I need an average of ten hours nightly, and if I do not get them over a long period then I do not feel good at all. On a race weekend I drain myself completely and inevitably fall short on sleep. What would be ideal would be to sleep right through the Monday and Tuesday after that, but in practice that cannot be done because we start off with tests again immediately or there are other jobs waiting to be done; so I end up dragging this sleep deficit around with me until I can really sleep right through a night again.

I never get tired during a Grand Prix, I never feel my body giving way during a race, so I am physically capable of meeting all the demands that are made on me without having to pay too much attention to keep-fit training. I pay far more attention to getting my proper ration of sleep, and I only go for a daily half-hour run when I do not feel tired any more. As there was scarcely a day in the 1975 season that I got all the sleep I needed, I hardly went running at all.

Obviously I try not to burn the candle at both ends. I do not smoke, never drink – except for something very small if I am really tempted, perhaps twice

With Günther Traub

Piloting the Cessna Golden Eagle

a year – and I am not a great partygoer. On a race weekend I go to the usual Marlborough dinner, but that is all. Nor do I like to go out, it does not do anything for me. I think most of the other Grand Prix drivers like a 'healthy' life as I do, there are not any playboys amongst us – because if you are a playboy you just will not be up to the job. Perhaps in earlier years it was different : there were not so many tests and trials then, and you had more spare time between races. But not now.

What I do regard as very sensible is a long training camp period. The last time I went in for one of these body-building programmes – it was early in the winter of 1974/5 at Saint Moritz – it was a very piecemeal affair and suffered accordingly, because I was able to keep at it say for three days, then I had to go off to Paris or Italy, I came back, had to go off again and so on. Under those circumstances the programme just did not work, because I used to get back to Saint Moritz dead tired and then just got tireder if I started right away with the sports again. I was working out there under the supervision of the former ice skating champion Günther Traub. I am sure that his programmes do you a lot of good – and his fees are correspondingly high.

My own hobby sport is skiing, and I am quite good at it. But I never really lose my fear of breaking a leg. There is no escape clause in my contract with them, but even so I would not like to see Ferrari's faces if I turned up just before the season began, wearing one leg in plaster. So I make a point of skiing particularly slowly if I can. For a while I manage, but then I find myself just picking up speed again. What I never do, however, is go skiing if the visibility is poor – then my fear of injury gets the upper hand.

It was Traub who suggested I should try long-distance skiing. I am sure it is good for your physique, but I found it all a crashing bore and do not go in for it any more.

There is a table-tennis outfit in a hall at our Fiorano test track, and the team go there for a game if we have time to kill. Not that it has done me any good, I am something of a rabbit at table tennis and easy meat for everybody else to beat. I have tried a bit of tennis – for instance in the tranquil days before the South African Grand Prix at the Kyalami ranch; I liked it a lot and I can well imagine that I would like to take it up seriously if ever I should get enough time to.

I have never been badly ill. Since I have been a professional, I have always taken great care not to catch a cold : from washing my hair, right down to the car's ventilation system – I adjust it so that it only gradually cools down.

By and large my attitude to my body is this : I try to live sensibly. The doctors tell me that this is the only reason that I managed to survive my crash on the Nürburgring.

IN THE MIDST OF LIFE

PUBLISHER'S NOTE

In August 1976 the author was so seriously injured in the German Grand Prix that for some days he hovered between life and death. On October 13th, 1976, he gave a remarkable interview to Harry Carpenter in the 'Sportsnight' programme on the BBC in which he described this disaster and its aftermath. We wish to thank the BBC for making a transcript of this interview available to us with permission to include it in this book.

In the Midst of Life

CARPENTER : But now, we come to motor-racing and the absorbing battle for the driver's world championship between James Hunt of Great Britain and Niki Lauda of Austria. Hunt's two wins in the last ten days, with one race to come, have given him a real chance of snatching the title from Lauda on the line. And one can understand British feelings running high for Hunt, who would be the first British world champion since Jackie Stewart. But there's much more to it than that. If you strip away all the legal wranglings, the protests, the disqualifications, the reinstatements, the bad feelings between McLaren and Ferrari, you are still left with the heart-wrenching story of Niki Lauda. These were the headlines and the grim pictures we woke up to the morning after the Olympic Games. Far from trying to retain his world championship, Lauda was now fighting for his life after being badly burned in a 150 mph crash in the German Grand Prix. His own story of how he came back to race again, in just six weeks, and today is still ahead in the drivers' championship is surely as moving an account to come out of sport in a very long time.

LAUDA : When I had the accident I must have got a big bang on my head and so I lost the memory for the last – I don't know – three minutes – and the following 20 minutes after the accident. The first thing I remember was the helicopter which was starting its engine and I asked where are we going and how long it takes me, because I said it takes 45 minutes to the hospital. That when I remember and from then on everything was working well again.

When I came to the hospital – you know you feel a kind of – you feel like you're very tired and you would like to go to sleep, but you know it's not just sleeping it's something else. And then you just fight with the brain. You hear noises, and you hear voices and you just try to listen, to what they are saying and you try to keep your brain working and to get the body ready to fight against illness, and I think this was very good and I did that because in that way I survived.

CARPENTER: You say it wasn't sleeping, it was something else? You mean you thought perhaps you were dying, did you?

LAUDA: You know that – no, you can feel that now everything is going wrong. You're getting weak and you feel you can't do anything.

CARPENTER: What was the thing that made you fight against it? What went on in your mind that said I've got to fight against this?

LAUDA: When that feeling came you get a big fright, you know you're really worried and frightened that you're going to die and that means you start everything possible to keep you going, and you can't start your body because your body doesn't react – you can only start your brain because you hear voices, you ask why, for example names – who is he and why is he not here and things just to keep the brain working and if the brain works the body starts to work, sooner or later.

CARPENTER: A priest came to see you, didn't he? Do you remember that?

LAUDA: Yes – er – one of the nurses asked me if I wanted a priest and I said yes, why not, because I was worried about everything, so I thought it might be a good idea. I'm Roman Catholic and so the priest came and I expected it that he would speak with me and tell me that, you know, that I should try hard to survive and all that, instead he didn't say anything, just put a little cross on my shoulder and left again. I don't know how the same in English is – the last . . . ?

CARPENTER: The Last Rites we say.

LAUDA: The Last Rites. And I didn't agree with that because I don't think this is the right way to do if a person is in the stage in what I was in. I think you should talk to him and at least try to help him, and make the Last Rites maybe so the guy doesn't feel, but not just come, make it and leave again.

CARPENTER: Part of your trouble apart from the facial damage – you had bad lung damage from inhaling the flames.

LAUDA: The worst was the lung damage because after the people told me a man can survive the lungs being in a stage that people say there's no way that they can come good again. And then suddenly from Thursday everything came good again.

CARPENTER: When did you realise that your face had been very badly burned?

LAUDA : They showed me a mirror I think Thursday or Friday and the burns wasn't the problem at that stage I had a head which was about three times as big as mine now – swollen up because of the 800 degrees I had for about 40 seconds, you know the body reacts and puts water in that place. I had a head which was as big as this. You know when I saw it I was a bit worried. That it might not go back again but the doctors told me that this is a normal reaction of the body and everything will go back to normal.

CARPENTER : Was it very difficult for you to accept that you had to show a face to the world that clearly was disfigured?

LAUDA : No. The worst thing was when I was in hospital – it was the other thing which really pissed me off I must say. But the journalists, especially they send special photographers for example from Paris, trying to get a picture of me. And they say you get so and so much money paid if you let your picture taken and all that. You know, I think if somebody has burns on his face or whatever through an accident – he's in problems, I think you have to respect the guy in that way, you don't just say 'listen, how does your face look?' You should treat him like an old person, I think, you should . . . how do you say in English.

CARPENTER : Pity? Sympathy?

LAUDA : Yes. Right. And this was very bad because they're just trying to get one picture of me with my burnt face and I got really upset about it and I just tried not to care because I think they shouldn't make money, newspapers, because of my face. So I had, for example the room in the hospital was always locked because everybody was worried that somebody would come in and for one second the nurse went out and left, and didn't lock the room and I was lying in bed because my hands had to be on the bed so I don't touch the face and I was lying there and suddenly a journalist came in – a photographer – with a machine and he ran off again and I couldn't do anything. I was lying there, you know, tied to the bed, and he took the picture, and left. But anyway this was the worst thing in this period and then I went home and there again I had the same problem that the house was surrounded by journalists just trying to take pictures. And then we just called the police and they cleared the place up. But this was very bad.

CARPENTER : Now how is it that you were able to come out of hospital and only six weeks in fact after that crash you got back into your car and you raced again in a Grand Prix event. I'd like to know what it was inside you that made you want to do that?

LAUDA : You know I like my job very much and I like the work with the cars – the technical side of it and motor racing I like. So I was thinking what is more important to me now is it the positive side or the negative side? And the positive side was still bigger and for me there was no question but to race again. The longer you stay out of racing the more the body goes down and the more you have to train again to come back. And then I was absolutely fit in Monza and this is the reason I went there, but I didn't want to go even half fit becasue I think it is very dangerous to do.

CARPENTER : Was there any fear that something similar might happen again?

LAUDA : No, it was very easy because on Friday we had very bad rain and it was raining a lot and I didn't feel, you know, like driving, because of aquaplaning. But then I told myself in that way you won't get back into motor racing if you sit in the pits, so you'd better get out and get used again to the car and get racing again. So I went out of the pits and did one lap quite slow in fourth gear only because there was so much rain and finally got aquaplaning in the straight which is when you drive in the rain quite normal. But I got such a fright suddenly you know when the car started to slide a bit that there was no way in which I could continue to drive. So I went back into the pits and said there is too much water for me and got out of the car. Sure there was a lot of water but the main problem was my brake was on, you know, in the brain. So I had no training on Friday and only one hour in the morning, for the grid positions. The first half of it was half wet, half damp and then you know I got going slowly and I told myself to get going now and not to be worried too much and I started to very slow, I didn't want – I didn't want to go flat out, I just went quicker and quicker slowly so everything, all my thinking could work with it. And then finally I think I was fifth quickest in the Ferrari team and everything was good again.

CARPENTER : So by some miracle Lauda was back, a lively ghost to haunt Britain's James Hunt who once again in this Italian Grand Prix, fell foul of authority and was relegated to the back of the grid. The amazing Lauda, close to death only six weeks earlier was fourth with Hunt nowhere. How can a man who suffered like Lauda force himself back into a car? Can he face danger in the same fearless way as before?

LAUDA : I think I get in the car the same way but I know that there are still to be . . . the same condition, you know, the same condition as I've been driving before, you know, absolutely on the limit, will take a while to get back to this stage because it's no good to just say I've had an accident and I try to forget it because he won't forget it. The thing is that you have to use your head and try to get through these problems – it means to try to understand first of all why the accident happened, if you want to go and race again – you know you have to think about all these things.

CARPENTER : Does a man, when he gets into a racing car, does a man change in some way, is he a different person when he gets behind the wheel than he is when he's just moving around normally?

LAUDA : Yes, because when you get in a racing car you have to, you know, press a button, press a switch because you have to just work on the car and not to get disturbed by any other thinking – you have to be 100 per cent concentrating – that means that you have to switch off all the rest, you know, and just concentrate on the driving, and when you get out the car you have to switch yourself back. And I think you've seen maybe some drivers who have had spins or accidents which they have no problems, they get out the car and they suddenly react completely crazy and they shout at people, they scream. And this is only because their mind and everything is still on racing through the accident or through the spin suddenly everything stopped. But the brain hasn't stopped, it's still thinking of driving, so he reacts from outside completely stupid, you know because he doesn't understand that he's now back in the real – in reality and walking back to the pits he shouts and screams you know, and then it takes a while. Some drivers, it takes I don't know – an hour to come back to the normal or another driver it takes 10 seconds, and he's normal.

CARPENTER : Can we now talk about the World Championship and the Grand Prix season which has been full of argument, disqualification and things like that. What is your impression – your views on the season so far?

LAUDA : My biggest opposition is James Hunt. And I think James – I like him very much – we work together very well in the past couple of races and everything was good. Even when the funny decision of Spain came which I think was completely wrong to give James the victory of Spain – when he drove an illegal car because if something is illegal it's out, if it's legal it's in. It's very simple. So I was never upset with him at that stage because I think it was the management of his car or the people who he worked with which made the mistake. Then came all the problems about Brands Hatch and there was another court case in Paris and suddenly the decision after Brands Hatch was for me. I don't want to discuss it whether it was wrong or right, the decision. At least I expected James to react in the same way – to respect me as a driver and fight if he wants against Ferrari. But what he did in the last two weeks – he's shouting and screaming at me and saying I'm completely wrong in what we did, you know, to make the protest and all that – I think that's really unfair because he should respect the other driver as a driver and nothing else. And that's what I do – I do my job to drive, he's doing his job. And for example we have a safety committee in the Grand Prix Drivers' Association which are five drivers which always sat together every year trying to improve the safety. And yesterday at 5 o'clock we had a meeting and I met James in the hotel and said come with me now, we'll be meeting in another hotel to discuss the safety and safety in future and he said I don't care if you have a safety committee, I'm here for racing and nothing else. I said, maybe I don't understand about you but you're a member of the safety committee why have you suddenly changed your mind and said 'I don't care about safety anymore, I care for racing?' I think that's wrong because if somebody works you should work the whole year even if the decision is against him and the decision at Brands Hatch sure is against James. I think he drove a very good race there but you know the judges in Paris said he was illegal in the race, therefore he was disqualified. I think he's changed a bit and it's not right what he did, because I think you should respect the sport as it is even if things are going wrong for him.

I think the most important thing in our sport is a lot of people criticise motor racing because they say no more sport is involved, they're only crazy people driving, they're high paid drivers driving the racing cars but I think there still is a sport because everybody is fighting with the same material for a World Championship. I think you respect the sport you have to respect the rules. And that's what McLaren didn't do. I think that's where they've been wrong. Because Ferrari, as long as I've been with them, we've never had any problems being legal or not.

CARPENTER : In these last ten days the race between Hunt and Lauda for the World Championship has hurried towards an almost unbelievable climax. Hunt has had two successive wins, in the Canadian Grand Prix at Mosport and last weekend in the American Grand Prix at Watkins Glen; now with just the Japanese Grand Prix to come Hunt is only three points behind but whatever happens, whoever wins the will to live of Niki Lauda is nothing less than a celebration of the human spirit.

LAUDA : I think in life you need a certain amount of luck but now the question is how much luck you need. I think the luck is the minimum part of it. I think it is, I think you can steer a lot of your life, you know, what I mean you have the wheel and you can do much more for yourself than a lot of people think.

CARPENTER : I've never in my life spoken to anyone with the iron-clad deter- mination of Niki Lauda, and whatever happens now, we surely have two winners. James Hunt has proved himself a great racing driver and Lauda a remarkable human being.